W9-BFU-380

Managing in a Team Environment

Managing in a Team Environment

John Robert Dew

QUORUM BOOKS
Westport, Connecticut • London

Library of Congress Cataloging-in-Publication Data

Dew, John R.
 Managing in a team environment / John Robert Dew.
  p.   cm.
 Includes bibliographical references and index.
 ISBN 1-56720-228-4 (alk. paper)
 1. Teams in the workplace—Management.   I. Title.
 HD66.D478   1998
 658.4′02—dc21   98-6018

British Library Cataloguing in Publication Data is available.

Library of Congress Catalog Card Number: 98-6018
ISBN: 1-56720-228-4

First published in 1998

Quorum Books, 88 Post Road West, Westport, CT 06881
An imprint of Greenwood Publishing Group, Inc.

Printed in the United States of America

The paper used in this book complies with the
Permanent Paper Standard issued by the National
Information Standards Organization (Z39.48-1984).

10 9 8 7 6 5 4 3 2 1

Contents

Introduction

Today many organizations are attempting to improve performance through the use of teams. Managing in a team environment requires a new set of skills and a new base of knowledge for success. Traditional management skills based on autocratic control and authority must give way to democratic skills used in consentaneous settings.

Organizations are attempting to use teams in two basic ways. First, cross-functional teams include people from a variety of departments in an organization to focus on solving a problem or improving a situation. Second, work groups, which transition into teams, where the manager's role changes to that of a facilitator or coach. In some cases the manager disappears altogether.

Cross-functional teams and cohesive work teams are both well-proven approaches for achieving dramatic improvement in almost any organizational setting. However, teams will inevitably challenge and erode autocratic management in organizations, just as representation in political systems conflicts with regencies, dictatorships, or control by a central committee in a totalitarian state.

Thousands of organizations in Europe and North America are moving toward workplace democracy, which will ultimately generate a crisis between democratic principles and the last vestige of autocracy—the workplace. The need to balance the interests of investors (or tax payers) with the desire for democratic processes within organizations will demand a new approach to leadership in most enterprises.

The drive toward creating team environments in the workplace arises from the fact that teams work. One case example from Ampex, an electronics company, aptly illustrates the reason that organizations are moving toward using more teams. Through the use of teams, Ampex has been able to cut inventory costs by 75 percent, reduce scrap and rework tenfold, increase on time delivery from 77 percent to 98 percent, and reduce the number of suppliers from 2,000 to 135 (Wellins et al., 1994).

The Ampex example has been repeated over and over again in numerous case studies of factories, schools, hospitals, and businesses that have become more effective, resilient, and adaptable to change when employee ideas are harnessed through the use of teams. As one senior manager at Xerox put it, "businesses are becoming companies of teams."

To hold onto these gains and continue to improve, teams must grow and function with an increasing awareness of the manner in which democratic processes work effectively in the office, shop floor, conference room, and hospital ward settings.

All of this boils down to a crisis for managers. With a few exceptions, most managers are accustomed to management thinking and behavior based on the premise that managers plan, lead, organize, and control. Now managers are being told to help their people work in teams that will plan, organize, control, and often lead. Old habits are hard to break, so the manager who has been asked to suddenly become a team leader is likely to fall back on more comfortable autocratic behaviors.

This book is designed to provide managers with the latest information on managing in a team environment. Academic resources will be cited, but the book is written to serve as a practical guide that describes specific actions that must be taken to achieve success in a team setting. Each chapter will cover important material related to teams and will include a section for managers who are serving as team leaders and middle managers who have multiple teams reporting to them.

This book is not designed to address issues related to the redesign of organizations and support systems to create the team environment. Readers interested in that subject should refer to *Empowerment and Democracy in the Workplace,* which addresses issues related to creating the team oriented work environment.

This book combines knowledge gained through academic studies with practical experience gained in managing in a team environment. The author has designed team processes at several facilites for Lockheed Martin Corporation, has taught many workshops on managing in the team environment, and has led many team endeavors. His most recent efforts in developing a team environment won Lockheed Martin recognition in 1997 from *Industry Week* magazine in their Best Plants in America competition. In addition, the author has consulted in the health care field, helping hospitals and other health organizations to manage their teams. The author also draws upon his experiences in teaching managers to lead in a team setting in city government.

1

Team Culture and Mission

There can be little doubt that the culture of an organization that is organized around teams is strikingly different from the culture of organizations that are organized in a traditional hierarchical fashion. Organizational culture consists of the standard sociological components, such as values, beliefs, mores, communication patterns, and distribution of power.

The differences between team culture and traditional culture are summarized in Table 1.1 and Table 1.2. These differences are drawn from observations of team and traditional cultures within Lockheed Martin through field observations and from published reports on team cultures at AT&T (Bloomquist and McClary, 1993) and at the Saturn plant (Bolton, 1993).

Table 1.1
Cultural Differences Related to Employee Norms and Behaviors

TRADITIONAL	TEAM
Not committed to organization's goals.	Participates in setting goals and shows commitment to goals.
Not involved in strategic planning and not aware of plans.	Represented or involved in strategic planning and aware of plans.
May or may not have useful job performance indicators.	Consistent presence of job performance indicators.
Management assigns work resulting in low ownership.	Employees divide up work and take ownership for tasks.
Enough work is done to get by and avoid discipline.	New levels of performance are set and consistently met.

Table 1.1 continued

TRADITIONAL	TEAM
Employees are unaware of the organization's economic health and do not care.	Books are open so employees know the organization's economic health and act accordingly.

The profound differences in employee knowledge and behavior in the team setting are created by changes in management behavior and also cause changes in management behavior. As in any complex system, interactions occur beyond a linear cause-and-effect relationship, leading to a synergistic effect.

Table 1.2
Cultural Differences Related to Management Norms and Behaviors

TRADITIONAL	TEAM
Managers plan, lead, organize, and control.	Managers lead the planning process, communicate, challenge, and maintain boundaries.
Managers spend a lot of time fighting crises.	Managers spend time identifying and removing system barriers.
Managers spend little time out on the floor with employees.	More management time is available to be with the employees.
Decisions are made quickly with a lot of time and energy spent overcoming resistance to change.	Decisions are made with more deliberation and implemented with greater ease.

WHAT'S NEW ABOUT TEAMS?

Actually, surprisingly little is new in our knowledge about teams and the benefits of team behaviors. Most of our knowledge about the benefits of teams was established in the 1940s and 1950s, but vigorously denied by managers who have been devoted to maintaining their power base in the workplace.

What is new is the gradual emergence of team-based companies as the best performing organizations in their class. Winners of the *Industry Week* magazine Best Plants in America contest have invariably built their low-cost, high-quality operations on team-based organizations. Companies that are winning the Malcolm Baldrige National Quality Award and are proven to outperform their competitors in return to investors, are also employing teams as the building blocks for success.

So, today we combine many decades of research and knowledge about teams with hard economic data that team-based organizations are superior to traditional hierarchical organizations in almost every facet.

CHANGING ETHICS

The gradual emergence of teams within the workplace denotes a subtle change in organizational ethics. Most organizations have traditionally adopted a teleological perspective in which the end justifies the means. From a teleological point of reference, an organization exists solely to achieve objectives and commonly assumes that the end objective is to produce a profit that is returned to the investors. Since profit is the motive, the organization will do whatever is necessary to make a profit. From this ethical perspective, managers are justified in doing whatever is necessary, such as using and abusing people, in the interest of achieving the organizational objectives. Human resources are a tool for management, along with capital, machinery, raw materials, and buildings.

With the emergence of teams we find a new ethical perspective starting to emerge. The new ethics are based on a deontological perspective that suggests that if we cannot achieve an objective through means we can accept, we should not strive toward that objective. Teamwork focuses on the humanistic value of men and women in the workplace who struggle together to achieve an objective.

This ethical issue of emphasis on means or on ends is really a central issue in this work. Each manager must struggle with the obligation to achieve objectives and to work within humanistic team-oriented boundaries. Fortunately, these are not mutually exclusive goals. In fact, as the performance of team-centered organizations shows, the best way to achieve the desired ends is through teams. The manager, however retains the responsibility and obligation to assure the success of the teams and the organization. The risk for the manager is to lead in a team setting without adopting an "anything goes," or laissez-faire attitude (Lewin, 1945). This concern will be addressed in each chapter with a set of observations that focus on both the role of the middle manager and the role of the front-line manager.

TO TEAM OR NOT TO TEAM?

A curious logic is currently being used to argue against the use of teams. It has been established that teams are highly beneficial in work groups that are performing complex tasks. A work group that is performing routine tasks under a supervisor may not show great improvement in performance by being reorganized as a team. Therefore, some people advocate maintaining the traditional structure.

This argument ignores the economic realities of organizations and the fact that forming teams can reduce costs. Although it is true that team performance of routine tasks may not always eclipse the traditional work group, the teams perform the work at a lower cost to the organization. Through the use of teams, organizations have reduced the number of front-line managers and middle managers, making the organization more competitive. At Miller

Brewing Company, for example, each front-line manager will now provide oversight for three teams of employees, giving a significant cost advantage to the team structure (Wellins, 1994).

CLARIFYING THE NEED FOR TEAMS

It is management's role to lead and communicate the need for the change from a traditional to a team-based culture. Regardless of whether the change process is gradual, with small pilot efforts, or wholesale with the complete redesign of the organizational structure, management must be providing leadership for the change effort.

Eastman Chemical Company (a Baldrige Award winner) has made this point in public presentations regarding its migration to a team culture (Wellins et al., 1994). In Eastman's experience, change must begin with the management's thinking and behaviors. Management must then make a compelling case for change to the whole organization. Management must guide the middle managers and front-line managers from directing to coaching in their day to day behaviors.

Above all, management must start the transition process by speaking to the organization about the mission of the organization and the related mission of each team.

CLARIFYING TEAM MISSIONS

Success in any venture requires all parts of an organization to be aligned with the rest of the organization in terms of their mission, vision, and actions. In a team environment, every team should have a mission statement that supports the overall mission of the enterprise. Every team member needs to know the mission of his or her team and the boundaries in which the team has to work to achieve its mission.

Start with a Charter

Effective organization of a team begins with a charter that defines the role of the team, the type of team structure, and the initial membership of the team. Team charters in Lockheed Martin's Utility Services organization define whether the team is a cross-functional team created to work on a specific project or an ongoing high-performance team of people who work around a particular product line or building. Charters define at least the initial members of the team, such as the immediate workers and representatives of support groups that are involved in a work process. Teams are often empowered to recruit more people as they see fit. Teams in the Xerox organization often include customers and suppliers as well as Xerox employees (Palmero and Watson, 1993).

Linkage to the Overall Mission

In a team environment, the manager must be able to articulate the organization's mission statement to the teams. Whether the organization is a hospital, factory, school, business, or government agency, a mission statement has probably been formulated. If not, the organization needs to develop one (Bean, 1993).

It is the manager's responsibility to promote the mission statement with the teams. Every team and every team member must understand that his or her purpose in the organization is to help achieve the organization's mission statement. Some teams will easily be able to identify with the organization's mission statement, while other teams may view their work as far removed in some type of support role.

Each team needs to develop its own mission statement in support of that of the overall organization. This is a vital starting point for every team. Understanding of the team's mission and how it supports the overall organization is a fundamental step in securing buy-in and commitment from team members to support the team's actions. The manager must emphasize the importance of each team doing its part for the overall organization to succeed.

At AT&T's microelectronics factory in Orlando, Florida for example, each team develops a mission statement that links the team to the company's overall mission (Gonnodo, 1997). Likewise, teams in Lockheed Martin have mission statements that connect the mission of the team with the mission of the factory in which the team works.

The manager must be careful not to jump ahead and attempt to define the mission statement for the team. People are more committed to a mission when they develop the mission statement themselves. Those who create tend to support.

Establishing Team Boundaries

All teams work within certain boundaries. These include being safe, working within procedures, protecting the environment, and working within some type of budget. Everyone in an enterprise is expected to be a good steward of the organization's budget, equipment, and resources.

The manager must reinforce the need for the organization to be safe and profitable. This often means sharing business and performance data with teams so they can identify with the performance of the organization as a whole. Managers must emphasize that when organizations operate in a safe and profitable manner, they can remain open, provide steady jobs, and provide a payroll for the workers.

In addition to helping each team define a team mission statement, the manager must also help them define a set of boundaries. These will vary greatly from organization to organization. Some teams are permitted to hire and fire; some are not. This must be defined as a boundary condition. Some teams conduct their own reviews of team members' performance; some do not. This must be defined as a boundary condition. All boundary conditions should be defined clearly and understood by the team members.

Teams at Lockheed Martin's Government Electronic Services plant in Moorestown, New Jersey all work within the following set of boundaries:

CAN	**CAN'T DO**
Understand your "customer's" needs.	Deviate from process/compliance.
Organize team, select members and leaders.	Hire/fire/discipline.
Determine objectives, create plan, and obtain support needed to reach work goals.	Choose vendors.
Assume responsibility for achieving work center performance objectives.	Change pay scale.
Control cost, manpower, work flow.	Refuse work.
Communicate thoroughly.	Be cost ineffective, adversely.
Impact schedule, quality, or integrity.	
Focus on the process and design.	
Improve or cross skills with training.	
Change layout of work center.	
Improve cycle time.	
Control schedule, work in progress, and material input.	
Recommend equipment changes.	

Over time a manager can expect that teams will test their boundaries and attempt to work on activities outside their boundaries. Managers should not be surprised when people want to exercise more control over their work life and should be prepared to either enforce the boundary or renegotiate it as appropriate.

Define the Team Mission Statement

One of the first steps in establishing a team is to define the team's specific mission statement. This should be a brief (one- or two-sentence) statement of the purpose of the team. The entire work group needs to work together to define the team mission statement. It needs to come from the team. It cannot be assigned to the team from management. The team will need to struggle and debate this to come up with a statement that really catches the core of what they are trying to do.

At one research facility, the crew of operators that runs the laboratory's steam plant decided to write a mission statement in their effort to become a team. They decided that their mission was to provide comfort to the researchers which meant that they would operate their building in such a manner that the temperature was always right in the laboratories across their site. A good mission statement goes beyond what the team does and may define the results that the team is producing. It should be linked in some way to the overall organization's mission statement.

Mission statements at Abbott Laboratories, for example, focus on developing shared responsibility for the team members, ownership of work processes, goals, accountability, vision, and commitment to the mission (Katkaveck and Mallamo, 1993).

Post the Mission Statement

One mistake that many organizations make is to file the mission statement away. Instead, it should be posted where everyone in the team, and anyone who comes in, can see it.

TEAM LEADER'S PERSPECTIVE

If you are the front-line manager of a group that is becoming a team, it is tempting to jump in and define the mission statement yourself. You probably know the team's work as well as anyone, and perhaps better than anyone else. However, if you define the mission statement, then you own it and the team members do not. It is much better to hold back and let the team come up with the mission statement so they will be committed to it.

MIDDLE MANAGER'S PERSPECTIVE

As the middle manager (with teams reporting to you) you have the responsibility for assuring that all your teams actually have a mission statement and that these statements are aligned with the overall organization's mission. You accomplish this through one of the key tools for managers in a team environment known as management by walking around. As you visit team work areas, check to see where the team's mission statements are posted. If they are not posted, find out whether they exist. If they do not exist, then insist that the team find time to develop their mission statement.

2

Ownership, Goal Setting, and Planning

Successful management in a team environment depends upon establishing a sense of ownership and commitment among the team members. Committed team members can accomplish almost anything, but people who are told they are a team and do not have a sense of ownership of their work or of their team process will accomplish little. Successful teams own their process and participate in setting team goals for performance and in planning how to achieve those goals.

OWNERSHIP

A team that has a mission statement is on the right path to developing a sense of ownership about the work they are performing. Each team plays a role that contributes to the overall success of the organization, and it is important that each team member recognize that role and have a sense of personal ownership and accountability for the team's work.

Sometimes people get very frustrated in doing their jobs because they must deal with difficult rules and complex regulations. Sometimes it seems that it is just too difficult to get things done. The risk that every individual team member runs is to stop taking ownership of the job and start acting like a victim. In fact, an entire team can take on a victim mentality that causes them to give up on their ability to control their own future.

Table 2.1 shows the levels of ownership for an individual and a team, ranging from a high sense of accountability to a low state of being a victim.

When individual and team behaviors are below the line in the middle of Table 2.1, people are acting as victims. When people allow themselves to act as victims, they will eventually become passive and will refuse to take any action that can improve their situation. Victim behaviors encourage more victim behavior. When individual and team behaviors are above the line in the middle of Table 2.1, people are taking ownership and accountability for what is going on around them. The success of a team based organization depends on the willingness of all individuals to be accountable and to not act as victims.

Table 2.1
Levels of Accountability

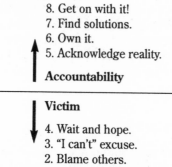

8. Get on with it!
7. Find solutions.
6. Own it.
5. Acknowledge reality.

Accountability

Victim

4. Wait and hope.
3. "I can't" excuse.
2. Blame others.
1. Unaware; unconscious.

SETTING GOALS

Some individuals are content to wallow in victimhood, refusing to acknowledge the reality of working in a competitive world. Managers must be willing to constantly confront teams with the hard evidence regarding the organization's performance and the requirements that each team must meet to support the overall organization.

Being successful in a competitive world usually does not mean that the team needs to work harder. Instead, it usually means that the team must work smarter (Simmons, 1995). Every team needs to set goals that focus on how the team is going to make improvements in the next twelve months. Every team needs to do this every year, and sometimes every six months to remain relevant and up to date. Improvements are actions that ensure that work is done with less effort, at lower cost, and in less time, and that enable the organization to sell a product or provide a service in a more competitive fashion and keep the organization economically healthy.

Team goals need to be focused on results, such as eliminating errors, doing a job in less time, reducing the amount of waste that is generated, reducing the amount of materials used to do a job, finding a safer way to get a job done, reducing scrap, or finding a better way to get a job done. Goals might include improving procedures, having better safety meetings, and improving communications with support groups or with the team's customers.

Who Sets the Team Goals?

Management must challenge each team to set high goals. However, the actual goals should be set by the team members after they have heard from management and fully understand what the whole organization is depending on them to do. Management must definitely express interest in the goals and can point out areas where improvement would help in achieving the overall organization's mission, but when it comes right down to it, the team must set its goals and the team members must be committed to the goals. For example, teams at the Tallahasee Democrat newspaper have been able to achieve high performance in accuracy, error reduction, and customer satisfaction because the newpaper's management allowed the teams to set their own goals (Katzenbach and Smith, 1993).

Once the team has agreed on its goals, the goals should be posted alongside the team's mission statement.

How High Should the Goals Be?

No team ever wins in sports by setting low goals. What would you think of a team that said its goal was to finish in the bottom half of its league? Time for a new coach!

Effective team goals are set at an absurdly high level. Do not shoot for marginal improvement and small gains. Challenge the teams to go with gusto for some goals that will require everyone to stretch. Having stretch goals encourages people to be creative, to get out of the box, and to find new and better ways to get things done. Ample evidence exists of teams that have improved performance by 100 percent and even 1,000 percent when encouraged to take ownership.

The key is to encourage absurdly high goals, to applaud and reward success, and not to harp on failure to meet the goals. For example, when the work teams at the Mine Safety Applicance Company were encouraged to set their own goals for producing batteries, they abandoned mangement's old goal of 300 per week and set an absurdly high goal of producing 450 batteries per week. They actually achieved 480 per week (Wellins et al., 1994).

Deming discouraged goal settings for a number of reasons. First, he observed that most goals were being set by the management, not by the employees, so there was little commitment to the goals. Without commitment goals become a burden instead of an inspiration. Deming also noted that most managers will set the goals far below what an organization is actually capable of doing. They do this to avoid being embarrassed and graded down on their annual performance review (Deming, 1986).

There is nothing wrong with setting goals when the team members do it and when the goals are used as an inspiring new level to reach and not as a weight to hold them down or to serve as a source of punishment if the goals are not reached.

PLANNING

Once the team has some good goals that will help it stretch, time must be invested in developing a plan regarding how the team will achieve its goals.

Effective team planning should include the following elements:

1. Clearly define what steps the team will take. This might include collecting data or consulting with customers or support organizations.
2. Define who on the team is going to perform each step.
3. Define when the work in each step is going to done and when it will be finished.
4. Define any special resources that the team will need in order to move ahead with the plan. Will there be a need for funding? If so, can the team show how there will be a return on the investment?

This planning needs to be carried out by all members of the team all working together at the same time. The team should write their plan on an easel pad where everyone can see and discuss it. The plan should be revised as much as necessary so that everyone in the team is committed to the overall plan and his or her specific role in the plan. Then, the plan should be posted alongside the mission statement and the goals so that the team can keep track of their progress during team meetings.

TEAM LEADER'S PERSPECTIVE

People who are in team leader positions are usually individuals who have been willing to take ownership and accountability and are willing to jump in and get a job done. The temptation will be to jump in and drive the goal-setting and planning process. The message that the team leader needs to send to the team is that he or she is interested in having high goals and effective plans, and is supportive of the team in developing the goals and plans. The team leader needs to have a voice in the process but must be careful not to dominate the process.

Autocratic behavior on the part of the team leader stimulates a victim response from the work force. When people are denied the opportunity to take a part in the planning process, they feel no ownership for the work goals and processes and slide down the scale into becoming victims.

MIDDLE MANAGER'S PERSPECTIVE

As you engage in managing by walking around, check your organization and determine whether people act and talk as if they are taking ownership or being victims. Make a poster of the accountability/victim chart and have each team post it in their work area and encourage people to discuss whether they are taking accountability or acting as victims. Ask to see each team's goals and plans. If a team does not have these in place, then encourage them to set aside the necessary time to get it done. If you ignore the lack of goals and plans in a team, then you are sending a message that says it must not really be important to have them and your team effort will fail.

More than anything else, the middle manager's role is to get the rocks out of the road for the teams. Team plans will often require resources to fix things that need improvement. The middle manager needs to be able to translate these specific operational issues into the language of money—return on investment—and get the resources required to support the team efforts.

On the other hand, the middle manager needs to make sure that each team fully understands the economic reality of the organization. If the budget is tight, then the teams need to acknowledge that reality and find solutions that make the best of the situation. Middle managers must not encourage teams to wait and hope for money to fix their problems. This will just reinforce the victim mentality.

3

Team Performance Indicators

In sports many indicators help a team assess its overall performance, such as runs batted in, number of time outs, number of foul shots, time spent in the penalty box, speed of a baseball pitch, or miles per minute of a long-distance runner. Of course, there is a bottom-line indicator in most sports as well. At the bottom line, we look at a team's score compared to its competitors. In racing, we look at the number of times a racing team wins. In track and field we measure the combined score of the whole team in all of the events.

Why do sports teams use indicators? In part, to determine who is a winner and who is not. But teams use the indicators to learn how to improve. Teams study the data from their games to figure out what to do better next time. The same is true for teams in the workplace. Just as in sports, work teams need to have performance indicators that give the team members feedback so they can continuously improve their function. It is management's responsibility to assure that every team has a set of indicators (Meyer, 1994).

Most businesses or organizations have some type of bottom-line indicators of performance. In a business this is usually a profit-or-loss statement. In government it may be adherence to a budget and data regarding the volume of service provided. In schools it may be the budget and performance on standardized tests. Management must track the bottom-line indicators and make decisions based on them.

It is essential for the teams in an organization to know what the bottom-line indicators are showing in terms of overall performance. Likewise, each team must have a set of indicators that will provide linkage between what the team is doing and how the organization as a whole is performing.

HOW FAST IS THE CAR GOING?

We're all used to having performance indicators around us when we do important tasks. For instance, consider the dashboard of your car. It is full of performance indicators that help you optimize your performance and stay out of trouble. You have a speedometer that tells you how fast you are going. This helps you to avoid getting speeding tickets, and it also helps you stay at the optimum legal speed when you are driving. You have special warning lights and noises that tell you if you have left your lights on, left your trunk open, or left on the emergency break. There are indicators to let you know which direction you have signaled for a turn and whether or not you have your bright lights on. All of these help you drive safely and get where you want to go. They help you achieve your driving mission and get the right results. You would not be successful driving with just one performance indicator on your dashboard.

Team Measures

Just like in sports or in driving a car, a team needs a set of performance indicators that give the team members feedback about their overall performance.

Finding the right set of measures for a team is never easy. It usually takes a lot of thinking and some trial and error. The important thing is to keep trying and to make the best use possible of the measures you have. Managers can push the process of developing performance indicators by encouraging each team to examine its mission statement. What is the mission of the team? Is there a way the team can measure the results they are going after? If so, then that needs to be one of their critical measures. Other important team measures exist just as there are multiple indicators on a dashboard. A team's safety performance must be measured. The team's overall attendance record at work is also vital. Some teams can track the cost of doing their business. Others can track the amount of work that is being done. Team data on training can be tracked as a performance indicator. Other performance indicators can come from the goals that the team has set. Accomplishment of the plans that the team has agreed on can be an important indicator for the team to use.

In many cases indicators can be expressed in numerical data. Other indicators can be color coded. For example, the material condition of workplaces can be color coded as green, yellow, or red, where green indicates good condition, yellow indicates some problems, and red indicates an unacceptable condition. Many indicators can be set up with green, yellow, and red coding.

Another way to generate indicators is to think in terms of things that are important to the team and things that are important to the team's customer(s). What data would the customer want the team to be tracking in regard to how they are providing services (Thor, 1990)?

The point of having performance indicators is to post them visibly where everyone on the team can see them and use them in making team decisions. The best way to gain agreement and understanding in a team is for everyone to have access to the same information. The performance indicators need to be the key ingredient in the team's regular meeting.

BALANCED-SCORECARD CONCEPT

In many team environments, management employs what is known as a balanced scorecard to track organizational and team performance. The balanced scorecard is a set of upper-level performance indicators that takes a balanced look at the organization's performance. It will usually include indicators that give feedback on customers' perceptions, quality of products or services, control of costs, regulatory performance, and other internal factors such as attendance or turnover rates. Often the balanced scorecard can be directly linked to the performance indicators at the team level. The ability to flow data up and down from the team to the boardroom is a powerful tool for team-based organizations.

Examples

Lockheed Martin's aerospace facility in Orlando, Florida makes outstanding use of performance indicators for its teams. Each team has an indicator board, which is a chalkboard on wheels with a photograph of the team members at the top of the board. Indicators vary from one team to the next, but most have a combination of numerical and color-coded indicators. The numerical indicators come directly from statistical process control charts that team members use to verify the quality of all the components they manufacture. The color-coded indicators, based on a green-yellow-red system, are for housekeeping, safety, scrap levels, and defects.

At Eastman the motto is "Feedback is the breakfast of champions" (Milliken, 1996). Eastman teams make use of posted visual performance indicators throughout the organization. Eastman's indicators include the baseline performance of a process for making comparisons. They also post past and current work period goals and the best-ever score for an indicator.

Performance indicators in work areas do not have to be fancy color coded, computer-generated documents. VIA Rail of Canada uses handmade performance indicators that are posted in maintenance shops and work areas (Bemowski, 1996). These indicators provide focus for teams and provide a reference point for discussion when managers visit work areas.

When Entergy Corporation began implementing natural work teams, they found that performance indicators were a major factor in success (Fleming, 1994). Ready-made indicators were not in place at Entergy, so teams had to roll up their sleeves and invent their own. These are often the best type of indicators since the people with their hands on the wheel are deciding what they need to see to drive the car.

Xerox uses storyboards to chart the progress of their work groups (Leo, 1996). Storyboards provide a balanced view of team performance, strengths, status of improvement areas, contributing factors to group performance, and status on actions.

At the Mayport Naval Station, teams use a variety of indicators to track their performance. Overall, the station tracks 118 indicators from production and service organizations and 51 indicators from support groups. Each team has its own set of indicators that feed into base wide indicators (Ryan, 1995).

At Wainwright Industries, a precision-stamping company in the automotive and aerospace industry, performance indicators were a key factor in mobilizing the company to win the Baldrige Award (Landes, 1995). Wainwright has a "mission control" room that is covered with status reports and color-coded indicators to give everyone in the company feedback on performance.

Federal Express collects companywide data on its internal process quality index and its external service quality index (Struebing, 1996). This performance data is fed back to employees on a weekly basis so that everyone knows how the organization is doing, and each team member can connect his or her efforts to the company's performance.

Teams at Texas Instruments develop their own performance indicators, looking at external customers' needs, the business owner's needs, and the needs of the work group (Struebing, 1996). Teams define their measures, develop methods for collecting raw data, and decide how the performance indicator data will be used. Texas Instrument's management uses a balanced-scorecard approach for top-level performance indicators and flows this information down to the work teams. The scorecard includes data on on-time delivery, defect reduction, cycle time, training hours, and revenue growth.

TEAM LEADER'S PERSPECTIVE

The team leader is often the creative source for team performance indicators. The team leader has had a lot of contact with upper management and with customers, so he or she can often develop a quick list of topics for performance indicators. While the team is in the process of developing indicators, it is usually best for the team leader to remain quiet at first and let the team members express their ideas. This builds team ownership and commitment to the indicators. Then, when the team has exhausted their ideas, the team leader should add the remaining indicators that he or she knows from experience will be beneficial.

Performance indicators give everyone in the team a level playing field in terms of knowledge about what is going on. Studies on conflict resolution have found that one of the best ways to resolve conflict is to be able to refer to fair and objective information. Performance indicators give the team this type of information, so when performance lags, the team leader has data to cite regarding the performance problems within the team.

MIDDLE MANAGER'S PERSPECTIVE

It is the middle manager's responsibility to assure that each team has a set of performance indicators in place. The middle managers should be aware of the types of data being tracked by each team. Where possible, there should be linkage between the team indicators and the indicators that the middle manager uses to guide his or her part of the organization.

The middle manager should observe the teams' performance indicators in the process of walking his or her spaces and be sure that the teams are keeping their indicators up to date.

Middle managers are the link between the team's performance indicators and the overall organization's performance-tracking system. It is the middle manager's role to flow down information from top level balanced scorecards to the team, and to feed team performance data into the management decision-making process.

4

Interdependence of Teams

Each team has a mission that contributes to the overall success of the whole organization. To accomplish that total mission the people in every team have to work together. Teams depend on each other for information, help, and support. Each team will depend on other teams for cooperation to get their work done, and each team will have other teams depending on them for cooperation.

The success of each team and the entire enterprise is based on people's willingness to work together and support one another (Cartwright and Lippett, 1957). An organization is interdependent, each part dependent on everyone else doing his or her part well. Trust is the key to interdependence. To be effective, team members have to trust each other and teams have to be able to trust other teams. Trust is the key, but trust is not easily given. It must be earned.

At the Saturn automotive plant, interdependence of work teams and effective horizontal integration of work activities has been identified as one of the most critical management issues in the effective use of teams (Bolton, 1993). Lockheed Martin managers working with teams and with shift organizations would certainly echo this observation.

BUILDING TRUST WITHIN TEAMS AND BETWEEN TEAMS

How do you tell whether there is trust in a workplace? Trust can be defined by the degree to which people are willing to share ideas, opinions, information; carry out agreements; and take risks without fear of being attacked, embarrassed, taken advantage of, or ridiculed.

In a low-trust environment people are not willing to share what they think or what they know. In low-trust settings people will not follow through on commitments and they will be unwilling to take risks that count on other people's performance.

High trust, on the other hand, allows people to share information and opinions, releasing positive energy in the whole organization. Trust makes it easier to identify problems and to fix them without fear.

A manager can do several things to build trust in the organization's teams.

1. Listen to what every person in the team has to say. Make sure the team members know that they are valued as members of the team.

2. Let people know that you are glad they are working together as a team and that they are part of that team. Trust grows when people are connected to a group.

3. Trust grows when people have a shared purpose. Involve everyone in the team in developing the mission statement and keep the mission statement posted for everyone to see.

4. Be committed to the goals the team has established. When people see that their management is committed to helping the teams be successful, they will begin to have confidence in their team process and in each other.

5. Encourage the teams to invest time in learning together and in team-building exercises.

THE EMOTIONAL BANK ACCOUNT

Every person in a team has an emotional bank account. When people listen to each other, share information, and follow through on commitments, they are making deposits in the emotional bank accounts they have with everyone on their team. When people do not listen to each other, do not share information with each other, and do not live up to their commitments, then they make withdrawals from the emotional bank accounts they have with others (Covey, 1989).

It is possible for people to drain their emotional bank accounts with everyone they know by being dishonest, rude, and treating others with contempt. This is true for people within a team as well as for managers in an organization. It is also possible for people to build up their emotional bank accounts with everyone they know by demonstrating caring behavior and being committed to people around them.

Team members need to listen to one another and support each other as much as possible. This builds up the deposits in the emotional bank accounts. When the emotional bank accounts are in good shape, it is easy for people to trust each other. When the accounts are drained, it will be difficult to have any trust.

Because team members spend a lot of time with one another, they can make a lot of withdrawals from their emotional bank accounts. It is important for managers to keep an eye on how the team members are treating each other and to be aware of what their own level of deposits and withdrawals may be from the teams in their organization.

WIN-WIN OPPORTUNITIES

Most relationships between people are either going to allow one person to win and one to lose, both to lose, or both to win. For example, if you have to do whatever someone tells you to do, that person may win and you may lose in terms of what gets done today at work. No one likes to lose, so the losing person will often try to make sure that nobody wins. A worker who resents being given orders may do a job poorly, so he and the supervisor both get in trouble. Sometimes one person will willingly lose so that the other person can win. This might be done in order to maintain a relationship, but it usually builds up resentment over time.

Win-win situations are those that allow everyone to win. Win-win opportunities are made possible when people trust each other and can count on others doing what they say they will do. Win-win opportunities also come about when management and employees can open the books and talk about the real economic condition of the workplace and the problems that need to be fixed (Fisher and Ury, 1981).

Teams offer an opportunity for win-win relationships. The employees win because they have more opportunity to exercise control over how their work is organized and conducted. Team members have more decision making authority. The organization wins because the employees are committed to do good work and will use their knowledge to make the organization more effective. This leads to lower costs, which can help market position and assure long-term stability in jobs. Managers win because they can demonstrate effective work performance without having to engage in stressful conflict that often leads to a lose-lose situation.

Commitment to the Team

In professional sports players get traded from one team to another. This sometimes creates problems with morale and commitment. No one wants to have a new player out on the field who is not 100 percent committed to winning. The same is true in a team environment at work. No one wants to work with someone who is not focused on the work and committed to the team's success, except perhaps other disgruntled people who want company in their misery. Focus and commitment put deposits in the emotional bank account of fellow team members. People make withdrawals when they say they are coming to work to rest up for the weekend or when they have nothing positive to say about the organization.

Trust comes when people know they can count on each other. People want to know that their team members will be there to do their job, and will be ready to support them when they need help, and are willing to follow through on commitments.

Performance Appraisals

The use and abuse of performance appraisal systems has been one of the key topics of discussion regarding quality improvement programs and teams over the past decades. Currently five clear paths are used by organizations to overcome the weaknesses associated with the traditional approach to individual performance appraisal that has been so clearly criticized by Deming.

One approach is to completely drop the appraisal of the individual's performance and rely solely on appraisal feedback for the team as a whole. Eastman has taken this approach by scrapping their old performance appraisal system and replacing it with team performance indicators. Team performance is tracked and the company places an emphasis on giving positive feedback to team performance. The Eastman approach places no limits on the number of teams that can be recognized as winners and makes every effort to expand the winner's circle. As one Eastman employee has commented, "Applause is like the accelerator to speed organizational improvement" (Milliken, 1996).

A second approach is to evaluate individuals based on a balanced-scorecard method. In this approach, the organization decides on a balance of work indicators that includes customer satisfaction, work on ongoing performance improvement, peer feedback, and participation in professional development and educational activities (Weber, 1995). At Wainwright Industries, a balanced-scorecard approach has replaced the traditional performance appraisal system. Everyone in the entire organization, from top to bottom, is evaluated on one set of five key indicators, including customer evaluations, support of company goals, and individual performance (Landes, 1995).

Some organizations are seeking to simplify the performance appraisal process by reducing it down to a basic checklist that each employee keeps to provide performance feedback (Sulzer-Azaroff and Harshbarger, 1995). The checklist approach gives the team member a set of indicators that he or she can check off on a card, such as attendance and product quality.

Other organizations are experimenting with 360 degree feedback systems. In this approach, the organization designs a formal evaluation form that is used in team settings (Rau, 1995). The team member gives the form to peers and customers, who complete it and return it to the individual. In some systems the evaluation form is completed and given to a human resources staff person or consultant who summarizes the data so that the individual will not know exactly which peer gave which comment.

Finally, in professional work settings, performance appraisals are being replaced by customer surveys and peer discussions (Fitzsimmons, 1996). In this approach, a person's customers are given a survey to complete that allows the customers to summarize the individual's performance. A trained peer collects the surveys, summarizes the data, and then conducts a discussion of the feedback with the individual.

Organizations will undoubtedly continue to experiment with methods for giving team members performance feedback. The overall objective of any system should be to improve performance and to build up deposits in the team member's emotional bank account.

Interdependence and Shift Work

Many factories and hospitals deal with around-the-clock operations that require shift work. Each shift may be a stand-alone organization, but it depends upon the preceding and following shifts also, so there is an issue of interdependence in this setting as well.

Sterling Winthrop, a pharmaceutical company, has had success in forming an entire shift organization as a single large team. Work groups within the shift function as subteams, but the team's identify is tied to its shift (Wellins et al., 1994). Special attention then needs to be given to effective shift turnover meetings as one shift leaves and another comes on.

TEAM LEADER'S PERSPECTIVE

The team leader has the responsibility to encourage people to put deposits into each other's emotional bank account. This is hard to do if the team leader's own account is overdrawn with the team members. The leader should build up the deposits in his or her account with team members by listening to them and helping with the team's efforts.

It is natural for people in the start-up phase of teams to express a great deal of skepticism about the team concept. Many people have years of negative experiences in the workplace, so they will not jump to give their trust to a new team initiative. This is especially true if earlier false efforts were touted for forming teams in the workplace, such as quality circles and workplace re-engineering fiascos. Team leaders build trust slowly, often using their own personal integrity and credibility to establish credibility for the organization as a whole.

MIDDLE MANAGER'S PERSPECTIVE

Extreme examples of high performance from teams are typically related to very high levels of commitment. One thousand percent performance improvements do happen when people in the workplace are motivated to win and are willing to overcome their differences in the interest of a common cause.

The middle manager plays a pivotal role in building up or tearing down the team structure. Middle managers who spend time out with the teams, who remove the rocks for the road so the teams can function, and who get rewards and recognition for their teams will be successful in steering the teams along a healthy journey.

5

Decision Making
and Team Dynamics

Work in a team environment requires involvement by the team members in making decisions. Not every decision needs to be made with the full involvement of a team. However, there needs to be agreement and understanding between management and the team members about what types of issues require full team discussion and what types of issues can be delegated to individual team members or retained by management.

Johnsonville's teams, for example, illustrate the type of decisions that teams are now making that used to be made only by managers. At Johnsonville teams ranging in size from five to twenty people make decisions to take on new products, purchase new machinery, and determine their daily production plans to meet their business goals (Dumaine, 1990).

How people make decisions and what they make decisions about often depend on how they see their overall situation. A team could spend a lot of time making a group decision about a relatively minor issue and allow major issues to go unaddressed, so it is important to begin the decision-making chapter by first looking at how teams can assess their circumstances. It is the manager's role to coach the teams in conducting thorough assessments to be confident that the teams are working on the most important issues and not wandering off on tangents.

ASSESSING THE CIRCUMSTANCES

Effective teams regularly invest time in assessing the circumstances around them. This means identifying the issues the team needs to be working on, prioritizing those issues, and then deciding what to do about each issue.

1. Identify the issues.
Teams should start by making a list of the issues that concern the team.

The list should be written on an easel pad or marker board where everyone can see the list as it is compiled. The team leader asks questions to help create the list, such as:

- What commitments does the team have to meet?
- What opportunities does the team have?
- What is the customer expecting the team to do?
- What changes can the team anticipate in the future?
- What requirements must the team meet?

2. Clarify the messy issues.

Sometimes a team member identifies an issue that is really a cluster of issues. Someone may say, "Our training needs improvement." That statement could include a number of specific issues that need to be addressed, such as record keeping, availability of classroom instruction, the quality of classroom instruction, or many other issues.

When a messy issue is placed on the list, the leader should ask the team to break it down into specific parts until they get to the point where they can see where specific actions could be taken to fix specific problems.

3. Agree on priorities.

Only a certain amount of time is available for a team to work on issues. Some things can be addressed right away and other things are going to have to wait a while before the team can get to them. Therefore, it is essential for the team to agree on priorities for the issues they have identified.

When a team sets priorities, they should ask three questions about each issue.

a. How serious is this issue? How will it impact safety, the environment, the operability of our equipment, our costs, or our customers' expectations?

b. How urgent is this issue? Do we have an immediate deadline or an immediate need to work on this now?

c. Will this issue get worse if we delay working on it now?

A team will want to work first on the most serious issues that have urgent deadlines and cannot be delayed. This is putting out the worst fires first. Over time the team may be able to eliminate the bad fires and concentrate on addressing issues that will have long term benefits but that are not urgent.

EXAMPLE

A team is beginning to look around and identify issues that need to be addressed. They make the following list of concerns and then prioritize them by seriousness, urgency, and growth. They give each item a high, medium, or low rating (H, M, L).

Issue	Seriousness	Urgency	Growth
Fix leak in safety shower.	M	M	H
Talk to customer about poor results on tests.	H	H	H
Find new way to conduct OSHA training.	L	M	M
Fix problem with computer database.	H	M	L

The team is going to put its first emphasis on talking to the customer about the poor results on tests. Then it can move on to fixing the problem with the computer data base and the leak in the safety shower. Eventually, the OSHA training will be improved as well.

The manager is responsible for checking in with the teams to make sure they have created a prioritized list of issues they are planning to work on. Without this type of list, teams will spend time on sporadic issues and will not have a sense of accomplishment. The priority list provides a good reference point for asking the team about what progress they are making. It can also serve as a focal point for team meetings to make sure the team is focusing its energy on the most important issues.

High-performance work teams at Lockheed Martin's Paducah plant consistently begin by conducting an assessment of their circumstances. This is sometimes an emotional experience because people are often strongly committed to making their work processes as effective as possible.

For example, a team of maintenance, operations, and engineering personnel was formed to improve the function of a chemical spray booth used to clean equipment. The team members began by listing all the issues that needed to be addressed, including maintenance work, procedures, permits, and equipment. Next, the team members looked at each issue to make sure it was adequately defined. In some cases, such as maintenance, they had to be more specific and list exactly what maintenance was needed. Then the team discussed priorities and agreed on them by looking at the relative seriousness of each item, the urgency of the item, and the problems associated with delaying each item. From this list the team developed an action plan and began to take control of their own destiny.

MAKING LOGICAL CHOICES

It is easier for teams to make decisions when people share a logical approach to making choices. A logical approach to making decisions allows people to be clear about the objectives they are trying to achieve, the choices they have for meeting their objectives, and the things that could go wrong with their choices.

HAVING CLEAR OBJECTIVES

When a team makes a decision it is made to accomplish some goal or objective. For example, if you decide to buy a boat, there are certain things you want to achieve. You may want to have a boat that allows you to go fishing. You may also want the boat to be used to take your kids out for water sports. Also, you may want to minimize the amount of money you are going to spend on this boat. These are all different objectives you want to achieve. It always helps to know what your objectives are.

Team decision making works well when people start by talking about what objectives they are trying to achieve. Clear consensus on the objectives makes it a lot easier to agree on which choice to make. However, if the team starts by debating the choices without having an understanding of what objectives are to be achieved, the team will be wasting its time and probably making withdrawals from emotional bank accounts.

One of the best things a manager can do in a team environment when teams are making decisions is to ask the team members to be clear about what their objectives are. Helping teams to be clear about their objectives will help them stay on target for making effective decisions.

HAVING CHOICES

After the team has agreed on the objectives, it is time to identify the options or choices from which the team can select. It is usually worth the time and effort to prepare a large field of options, so nobody feels that a particular option was railroaded through the team.

Choices can come from a variety of places depending on the issue at hand. They could be options provided by vendors, information from technical journals, or data from any of a hundred other sources.

The team should compare the options to the objectives they want to achieve and decide which choice does the best job of meeting the objectives.

COMPLICATED CHOICES

Sometimes it is not immediately clear to the team which option does the best job in meeting the objectives. For example, in buying a boat one boat may be best for fishing but another may be best for water sports. Most team decisions are not complicated and do not require additional structure, but when a team has a tough issue, the manager needs to know how to advise the team of a structured way to take care of the situation.

When making complicated choices, the team needs to prioritize the objectives it is trying to achieve. Through discussion the team should decide which objective is the most important. This will be very helpful in comparing the choices. The best choice will be the one that helps achieve the most important objectives.

Some objectives are so important that the team may require the choices to meet them. For instance, you may have four children in your family who all want to go out on the boat. The boat must be large enough to carry all four of the children. That will rule out some small boats as options. Again, reaching consensus first about the objectives and the relative importance of the objectives is the best first step to making a complicated team decision (Kaye, 1992).

The team can give weights to the options to show how well each option meets the objective. Give the choice that best meets an objective a score of 10. Give other options scores relative to the best choice on a scale of 10 down to 0. There will be a lot of discussion within the team at this point.

It is important to place the work on an easel pad for the whole team to be able to see as it evolves. The easel should state the decision that is being made, show the objectives to be achieved, show which objectives are musts, indicate the relative importance of the objectives, show the choices that are available, and show how well each option meets the objectives.

EXAMPLE

Decision: Select the best nurse to promote to team leader.

Objectives		Choices			
	Weight	Rose	Alice	Ken	Sally
Communication skills	8	x 6 = 48	x 9 = 72	x10 = 80	x 4 = 32
Technical knowledge	10	x 8 = 80	x10 =100	x 8 = 80	x 6 = 60
Organizational skills	6	x 8 = 48	x10 = 60	x 4 = 32	x 8 = 48
Total of weight x score		176	232	192	140

Each objective receives a weight so that the more important objectives are given the greatest emphasis. Each choice receives a score on how it performs on each objective. The choices are scored in comparison to one another, with the choice that does the best job being anchored at a score of 10. All other choices are relative to 10. After each choice has been evaluated for each objective, multiply the weight times the score to determine the weighted score for each choice on each objective, then total the weighted scores. This approach offers the advantage of having a clear and visible process that everyone on the team can follow and participate in.

WHAT CAN GO WRONG?

Before you make a final decision and start to take actions and commit resources, it is always a good idea to ask what can go wrong. In the boating example, we might ask whether we can get service for the boat we chose in our geographical area. Can we tow it and can we store it? Asking what can go wrong is the best way to ensure that the team's efforts are successful.

It is the manager's role to encourage the team to ask itself what can go wrong with the decisions it makes. This is an important audit point for the manager. When the manager asks the team if they have considered what can go wrong with their decision or their plan of action and the team shows evidence that they have thought this through, then the manager can back off and allow the team to proceed. If the team's response indicates that they have not fully considered what could go wrong, then the manager needs to coach the team on considering the downside of their decisions and plans.

If the team members or management are making it difficult to ask the question of what can go wrong, then the organization is headed for major problems. The classic problem of tightly knit teams is called "group think" (Janis, 1972). In group think, team members are discouraged from asking questions or taking positions that might rock the boat. Asking questions and pointing out problems is interpreted as being disloyal to the team.

If a team is discouraging its members from asking what can go wrong, it is time for the manager to call time-out and to lead the team in self-assessment to help them out of this problem (see suggestions in Chapter 9).

NOMINAL GROUP TECHNIQUE

Nominal group technique (NGT) is another quick way to help teams make decisions (Mosley, 1974). This method will promote discussion but it also minimizes debates and stalemates. It is also different from majority rule. The following are steps in the nominal group technique:

1. Start by being clear what the issue is that requires a decision. Encourage the team to be clear about the objectives that need to be satisfied in making the decision.

2. List the options on an easel where everyone can see them.

3. Give each option a letter so it can be easily identified (a, b, c, etc.).

4. Give team members a few minutes to discuss the options and let people voice their opinions as to the pros and cons of the options.

5. Allow each person to prioritize the options by writing down the rank order of the items on the list. Suppose there are twelve choices. Each person makes a ranked list of 5, 4, 3, 2, 1. A rank of 5 is the person's first choice and gives 5 points to that choice. A rank of 4 is next in preference and gives 4 points, etc.

6. Each person's ranking is tallied to give a composite score of how the team

members individually ranked the issues. This is done quickly, without argument, and each person makes his or her choice in private, so the team members do not have to be concerned about what others in the team may think about their choices.

The highest-scoring choice may not have been everyone's first choice, but in many cases, the highest-scoring choice was in most team members' top three.

If the team is working on a major process where they need to chose from among twenty or more alternatives, the process can be speeded up by placing the choices on easel paper and giving each participant a number of colored stickers. Everyone gets up and places one sticker by his or her top choice. This provides the group with an immediate forced ranking of the choices. This approach is not as private as the secret ballot, but it is fast.

THE MEANING OF CONSENSUS

Consensus in a team is not the same thing as majority rule. In majority rule there are a majority who "wins" and a minority who "loses." Voting can be a clear and quick way to reach a decision, but it sometimes leaves people with the feeling that they have been defeated, and they may not be supportive in implementing the decision that has been reached.

Political democracy relies on voting and majority rule, but organizational democracy relies on developing consensus in which people will consent to work together.

Consensus decision making has the following characteristics that are different from majority rule and from hiearchical decision making:

1. There is an emphasis on dialogue and understanding other people's points of view.

2. People are encourage to generate many options, and even invent new options as they go along.

3. The objective is a win-win outcome, not win-lose.

4. Everyone can "buy in" at least 70 percent with the decision that is made.

5. No one ends up with serious heartburn over the decision.

The teams at General Motors' Saturn plant use consensus decision making in which "consensus is achieved when everyone (not the majority) is 70 percent comfortable with a decision and 100% committed to its implementation" (Bolton, 1993).

Do all decisions in a team environment need to be reached by consensus? Absolutely not. What the team needs is a consensus about which decisions should be discussed by the whole team and which ones can be made by individuals. For example, if a team member is designated as being responsible for conducting safety meetings, that person should be able to make the choices about the content of the safety meetings

TEAM LEADER'S PERSPECTIVE

Gaining a consensus about which issues require team participation and which issues are delegated to team members or retained by the team leader is a fundamental issue. The faster this agreement is clarified and established, the sooner the team will function effectively. This consensus about decision making can certainly be renegotiated over time as the team matures. A lack of agreement about decision making will erode the trust within the team.

The risk that front-line managers run is the abdication of their role in team decision making. The manager is a member of the team and his or her opinion counts too. The manager should not absent himself from team decision-making meetings unless he has a particular reason for not having his voice heard. The manager's participation in the decision making process is delicate. His voice must be heard, but it must not dominate the team.

MIDDLE MANAGER'S PERSPECTIVE

As the manager sits in on team meetings, he or she will want to audit several points related to decision making. Are the teams considering a full range of choices or are they jumping to one choice and not fully considering the range of options? Are team members avoiding voicing differing opinions and sliding toward group think? Are team members asking the critical questions about what could go wrong with their decisions?

When sitting in on team meetings, the middle manager should participate by adding information. If he thinks the team is not doing an adequate job of consensus decision making, he should express his concerns. He should not pull any punches or sugar coat his opinions about how the team is performing. The manager should state his views and then give the team some time to think about how it wants to respond.

6

Understanding
and Being Understood
Within a Team Culture

Every team in the organization has an important role to play in the overall success of the enterprise and every person on the team can make an important contribution to the team's success. There are no unimportant jobs or unimportant people. We all want to be valued for our contributions and we all want to be understood for the value we add to the organization. The best way to be understood is to understand others and to act in a mature manner as adults.

While this may not sound like a hard hitting part of effective management of teams, most successful team-oriented organizations pay attention to this issue. Wallace Corporation, for instance (winner of the 1990 Baldrige Award), invests in teaching its associates ways to recognize and use various social styles in work interactions (Gilbert, 1991). Training in social styles and diversity is a consistent theme as well throughout the Lockheed Martin organization and is essential for enabling teams to function. The Appendix to this chapter includes a useful instrument for evaluating each team member's approach to participation in the team.

VALUING DIFFERENCES

We start understanding others and ourselves by accepting the fact that all people are different and that these differences are a source of strength in the workplace. Not everyone around you is going to be just like you, so your contribution is special.

There are all kinds of differences between people in the workplace. Let's take a quick look at a few of the most obvious differences that influence how people behave and the special things they bring to the team.

Life Stages

People in your team will be of different ages. Age itself usually has little to do with work performance, but as people age they typically go through various life stages that influence how they view work (Bee, 1987).

Young adults are dealing with issues such as finding a significant partner for life and starting a family. Young adults are dealing with the economic challenge of accumulating household items and buying their first home and they are often trying to improve their careers or job skills by going to school in addition to being at work.

Middle adults are dealing with family issues, often with young children and adolescent children. Demands from outside of work are great from the community and from the family. Middle adults usually have good health and maturity, but sometimes make major midlife changes, such as starting new careers or new families.

Mature adults are dealing with family challenges as well as career challenges. By the time a people reach their fifties, they are dealing with adolescent children or young adults they are helping launch into school or into work. The mature adult also is dealing with aging parents, beginning plans for retirement, and often feels the greatest need for secure and predictable employment and income.

Where you are in the adult life cycle will influence how you see work, your willingness to put in extra effort to support work goals, and the type of support you need from your fellow team members.

Family Position

Many psychologists think we are strongly influenced by our birth order in our families. Were you the first child in your family, expected to take responsibility for your younger brothers and sisters? Do you still act like the oldest sibling in your team? Were you the baby of the family, used to being cared for by parents and older brothers or sisters? Is that the way you view your team at work? Were you a middle child, giving and receiving care, but sandwiched somewhere in the middle?

Ethnic Background

Every person comes from some sort of ethnic background. This means that there were values and beliefs in the family that each person was taught as a child. Each person has set of beliefs about what is right and wrong, good and bad, normal and not normal that was learned in childhood. People learn to enjoy certain foods, celebrate certain holidays, and value certain beliefs based on the ethnic background of their families. Attitudes about work and trust are also learned at an early age in our families.

Knowledge

Everybody is smart about something. Some people have great intelligence in figuring out how to fix things and using mechanical skills and tools. Others are smart about mathematics, number skills, and science. Some are gifted with language skills; others learn to do a certain job better than anyone else. Each of us has had different experiences in school—good teachers or bad teachers who inspired us or turned us off, strengths in different subjects, and weaknesses too. Our differences in education and experience mean that we all bring something important to the team. The knowledge of the team is increased by every team member, if we will recognize and value the knowledge that other people bring. The synergy that develops from combining the knowledge of people from a variety of backgrounds can tremendously increase the productivity and performance of an organization when each individual's knowledge is valued.

Thinking

Different people have different thinking patterns. Some people rely on highly rational thinking, primarily using the left side of their brain. Other people think in terms of patterns, and relationships, using primarily the right side of their brain. Some people think in a mixture of left-brain and right-brain styles (Herrmann, 1996).

Left-brain and right-brain thinking styles mean that people will organize information differently. Left-brain thinkers will want a team's activities to be orderly and plans to be prepared in a logical manner. Right-brain thinkers will be more comfortable with the team making more spontaneous decisions. Left-brain thinkers will encourage the team to have clear measures of performance while right-brain thinkers may encourage the team to get out and talk to the customers. In problem solving, the left-brain thinkers will prefer the systematic collection of data and the use of statistical tools to determine causes. The right-brain thinkers will prefer the use of visual tools that show the relationship of work issues, such as cause-and-effect diagrams and flow diagrams.

Interests

Different people acquire different interests and hobbies that create common bonds with other people. You may feel closer to people who share your interest in sports, hunting, craftwork, food, or reading. Other people may have interests that do not appeal to you and seem a waste of time. Our interests are often learned from family members or closely related to how we think. Interests change as people move through their life cycle. Interests can bring people together or divide them.

Personality Types

The psychologist Carl Jung had a theory that there are basic types of personalities that people develop in their lives. These personalities are shaped by many of the factors that have been listed above, such as family position, early childhood experiences, and perhaps biological imprinting from your ancestors.

When you look at a team of people, you often find that they have different ways of acting in the team and in response to the situations that they encounter. No personality style is right or wrong, or good or bad. Personalities are just different, and these differences can bring strength to a team.

The four basic personality styles are intuitor, thinker, feeler, and senser. The intuitor is often focused on the future, is concerned with concepts, probably reads a lot, and likes to think a problem through, using his or her imagination. The thinker wants to think things through and probably wants to have background information. Thinkers like to be organized, to have data, to consider alternatives, and to not be rushed into doing things. The feeler enjoys dealing with people on a personal basis, like talking over an issue while sharing a cup of coffee. Feelers are concerned with how people will react and build on personal relationships to get things done. The senser is sometimes refered to as a driver, because he or she likes to get things done, to be brief and focused. Sensers want to know what the bottom line is, being practical and not spending time on a lot of alternatives. The senser likes to be brief.

A team might include a senser who wants to get to the bottom line and make a decision, a thinker who wants to have more data and consider the alternatives, a feeler who wants to get everybody together to talk about the problem, and an intuitor who may have an idea about how fixing this problem might open up new possibilities for the team.

Here's the rub. If you are a senser and want to get things done, you have to learn to value the input of the others. If you are an intuitor, you have to value the senser's insistence on getting things done. If you are a thinker, you have to value the people perspective from feelers and the bottom-line focus of sensers. If you are a feeler, you have to appreciate the strengths brought to the team by the other personality types.

What is your style? A personality indicator instrument called *I Speak Your Language,* published by Drake Beam Morin, can help you understand yourself better. Other instruments are also on the market based on similar principles and research. All of these instruments can help people better understand themselves and better understand the strengths that diversity brings to a team. However, the use of these instruments within a hierarchical organizational structure has little proven value and may become yet another tool for manipulation within a teleological ethical perspective.

The Village Idiot

Some people who study teams and work groups find that there is a close similarity between work groups and small villages. Everyone knows everyone else and people are mutually interdependent for support. Occasionally a village will have an idiot. Over time this term has taken on many meanings, but the original meaning of idiot is a person who is focused only on himself or herself. The word comes from the Greek word *idios,* meaning being focused on yourself. When you are focused on yourself and not paying attention to other people, when you only value your own point of view and do not listen to others, you are being an idiot.

Abundance or Scarcity?

One of the reasons people are sometimes unwilling to accept or value differences in other people has to do with how they see the world. Some people view the world from a perspective of scarcity. They think there is only a limited amount of time, attention, or resources and they want to make sure they get their share, regardless of what happens to other people. If you work from a perspective of scarcity, then you will resent other people who are recognized for success and will envy the good things that happen to people around you. In the long run, the perspective of scarcity leads to personal disappointment and allows people to justify doing almost anything to get what they want (Covey, 1989).

In a successful organization, people learn to adopt a perspective of abundance. There is plenty of recognition to go around and we can have a win-win approach. When the team is successful, it helps the whole organization to succeed. When the organization succeeds, the rewards can be shared and careers can advance. Operating from a perspective of abundance, we want other people to succeed and we want to be part of a winning team.

Imagine a sports team where the team players are jealous of each other whenever they make a good play. On a winning team, the team members cheer each other on with every good play, because they know that there is an abundance of rewards for being on a winning team.

BEING A MATURE TEAM PLAYER

A team can have good coaching, good performance indicators, clear goals, and the resources to do the job. But the bottom line factor in team success is the commitment of the team members to work together as mature adults. Maturity will allow a team to overcome all obstacles. Without maturity, even the most intelligent individuals with the greatest resources will fail. Maturity is the willingness to act as adults and be responsible for our behavior. When we are mature, we have the courage to do what needs to be done and we are considerate regarding the needs of the other people around us. The mature team player knows when to pass the ball to another team member who has a better chance at making a score and is glad when the other team member makes the score for the team.

LISTENING SKILLS

One of the key factors in the success of any team is the degree to which team members communicate effectively with each other. Many things can mess up communication within a team. Someone may decide not to share information, or the team may become too busy "getting things done" to commmunicate until the team starts to fall apart.

One common problem with communication in teams, and in other settings, is the failure to effectively listen to one another. There are all sorts of barriers to effective listening, including the following (Rogers, 1961):

1. We value our own ideas above those of others, so we don't listen to what other people have to say.

2. We are impatient and want to get on with making a decision or solving a problem (with our own answer).

3. We think that our own experience or our own education means we know more than other people, so we don't bother listening to them.

4. We don't know how to listen.

Good listening is the key to cooperation, mutual respect, and conflict resolution in any situation. When someone is speaking to us, they are always communicating two messages at the same time. One message is the *factual information* they want to get across to us. The second message is *their feelings* about the situation. It is important to listen to both *facts* and *feelings* to be a good listener.

If you listen to someone and hear the facts but ignore the feelings, that person will believe you did not listen to him. Feelings are often expressed through tone of voice, inflection, and facial expressions. This means that when we listen, we have to listen with our eyes and our ears, which makes communication over the telephone even more difficult than face to face communication.

The best way to know that you understand what someone has said is to repeat back to them the facts and the feelings you have heard. For example, if someone is upset because you did not meet a deadline to get a job done, acknowledge his anger or disappointment at the same time you talk about how to get the job completed. Reflecting back facts and feelings is a good way to listen and good listening puts a deposit in your emotional bank account with the other person.

EFFECTIVE WORKPLACE COMMUNICATION

When we communicate with each other in the workplace, we often do only half the job and then act like a victim when things don't get finished. We may say, "I left a note on his desk," or "I sent him an e-mail message," as if that is all we needed to do and it is not our fault that the other person didn't follow through.

Effective communication means making sure that your information got through to the other person, was understood, and was acted on. Here is a checklist of questions to ask yourself to make sure your communication was effective:

1. Whom did you call?

2. What did you say?

3. When did you say it?

4. What did you agree on?

5. What is the next step?

6. Who else needs to know?

If you will ask yourself these questions and provide yourself with good answers you will be functioning high on the scale of accountability and staying out of the victim zone.

TEAM SELF-ASSESSMENTS

Effective teams occasionally take time out to do a quick self-assessment to see how well they are functioning. A good self-assessment will look at how the team is doing on task and maintenance functions (Jenkins, 1948).

Self-assessments can be done by asking a series of questions that everyone in the group discusses. Good questions to ask include:

1. How far do we get in our meetings? Do we cover the whole agenda?

2. Are we all clear on our goals? Does everyone support the goals?

3. To what extent do we have problems due to lack of information?

4. Are we all equally interested in what the team is trying to do?

5. Does the team feel united by a common interest?

6. What kinds of conflicts get in the way of achieving our common goal?

7. Do people believe it is okay to express a different opinion?

8. Are team members cooperative or competitive?

9. Is participation something that everyone on the team does or do just one or two people do all the talking?

10. Do people's comments indicate that they are listening to each other?

11. Is the group working with good data or with hunches and beliefs?

12. How well is the team doing on meeting its goals?

13. Are performance indicators kept up to date and used by the team?

14. Are team members open and honest in giving each other feedback?

15. What is the status of the emotional bank accounts in the team?

16. Does the team do an effective job of celebrating its successes?

17. Are the team's customers pleased with the team's performance?

18. Is the team working well with other work groups?

Sometimes it is a good idea for teams to use an end-of-the-meeting suggestion slip to get feedback about how the team is working. Here's an example:

What did you think of this team meeting?
Your comments can help the team do better.

1. How did you feel about this meeting? (circle one)

No good   Mediocre   All right   Good   Very good

2. What are the weaknesses? _____

_____

_____

3. What are the strong points? _____

_____

_____

4. What improvements would you suggest? _____

_____

_____

If we are willing to ask ourselves questions and constantly seek to improve the way we work together, we will succeed in our goals. If we are unwilling to critically reflect on how we work together, we will eventually run into trouble.

TEAM LEADER'S PERSPECTIVE

The team leader serves as the coach for the team on the issues of understanding and being understood. The team leader will often serve as the interface with other teams, so he or she carries an extra burden for the team of being aware of establishing and maintaining a healthy emotional bank account with other teams.

MIDDLE MANAGER'S PERSPECTIVE

The middle manager's role is to encourage the people in the organization to listen to each other and to communicate effectively. When the manager sits in on team meetings, he or she should listen to how the team deals with communication issues and should coach them on how to improve. The middle manager should champion the selection of some type of personality profile indicator that can be used throughout his or her organization, such as the Myers-Briggs instrument, Wilson Learning's *Managing Interpersonal Relations,* or Drake Beam Morin's *I Speak Your Language.* The middle manager needs to place some boundaries on the use of personality indicators. If each team selects their own assessment tool, there will be no synergy created by exchanging assessment data consistently across team boundaries. It is a good idea to select one assessment instrument and stick with it for several years across a large part of the organization.

APPENDIX

Team Participation Profile

People have different expectations and interests when working in a team setting. This instrument is designed to give you feedback on the manner in which you approach work in a team setting. The instrument also provides insights into how other people may approach team work in a different manner from you. Understanding your own style for working in a team, as well as the different styles of others in your team, will help your team function more effectively.

INSTRUCTIONS

This instrument consists of thirty pairs of statements. For each pair, select the statement that comes closest to describing your own belief or behavior concerning team activities. There may be some pairs in which neither of the statements is quite like you. If so, please select the choice that is most like you. Please make your selections based on how you actually behave and feel in your team or group setting. Do not make your choice based on how you think you ought to behave, but based on how you actually behave, think, and feel.

1. A. The best meetings focus on completing all the items on the agenda.
   B. The best meetings focus on hearing what everyone has to say.

2. A. The best meetings occur when you have the right information available to make a good decision.
   B. The best meetings occur when you look for creative ways to get things done.

3. A. During meetings, I like to cut to the chase, get to the bottom line, and get things done.
   B. During meetings, I like to identify all the issues, prioritize them, and use brainstorming to come up with answers.

4. A. I am most likely to bring some snacks to a meeting to share with everyone.
   B. I am most likely to bring magic markers to a meeting so we can use the flipcharts.

5. A. In a meeting, I am most likely to listen to peoples' ideas and work with them to find the best answer to our situation.
   B. In a meeting, I want to make the best decision based on the data we have available.

6. A. In a meeting, we should take the time to get all the facts out before we make a decision.
   B. In a meeting, we should do something to stimulate creative thinking.

7. A. The best meetings focus on completing all the items on the agenda.
   B. The best meetings occur when you look for creative ways to get things done.

8. A. I am bothered when I see someone is not being listened to in a meeting.
   B. I am bothered if we do not take the time to study the data to get the best answer.

9. A. I am most likely to bring information about goals and deadlines to a meeting.
   B. I am most likely to bring some snacks to a meeting to share with everyone.

10. A. I am bothered when we have lengthy discussions in a meeting.
    B. We should take whatever time is necessary to get all the right information before we make a decision.

11. A. I prefer to listen to everyone's ideas and come up with the best decision or plan.
    B. I prefer to study the problem, probably using some type of flow chart or diagram, and find an answer to the problem.

12. A. During meetings, I like to cut to the chase, get to the bottom line, and get things done.
    B. During meetings, I prefer to study the data and make a decision based on the data.

13. A. I am most likely to bring charts, graphs, and printouts to a meeting so we will have some meaningful data.
    B. I am most likely to bring magic markers to a meeting so we can use the flipcharts.

14. A. When confronted with a problem, I want to be realistic, find an answer, and
       get the job done.
    B. When confronted with a problem, I want to make the right decision based
       on the facts and data I can find.

15. A. I get frustrated when people take a lot of time during a meeting to express
       their views.
    B. I am willing to listen to what people have to say, whether it is in the work-
       place, or in a meeting.

16. A. The best meetings focus on completing all the items on the agenda.
    B. The best meetings occur when you have the right information available to
       make a good decision.

17. A. During meetings, we should take the time to study the data to get the best
       answer.
    B. During meetings, I like to identify all the issues, prioritize them, and use
       brainstorming to come up with answers.

18. A. When solving a problem or making a plan, I like to get everyone's input on
       what we should do.
    B. When solving a problem or making a plan, I like to do something to stimu-
       late people to have creative ideas.

19. A. I am most likely to bring information about goals and deadlines to a meet-
       ing.
    B. I am most likely to bring magic markers to a meeting so we can use the
       flipcharts.

20. A. When confronted with a problem, I want to be realistic, find an answer, and
       get the job done.
    B. When confronted with a problem, I want to take the time to hear every-
       one's information and opinion about what we should do.

21. A. The best meetings focus on hearing what everyone has to say.
    B. The best meetings occur when you have the right information available to
       make a good decision.

22. A. During meetings, I like to cut to the chase, get to the bottom line, and get
       things done.
    B. I am bothered when I see someone is not being listened to in a meeting.

23. A. I get frustrated when people take a lot of time during a meeting to express
       their views.
    B. In a meeting, we should do something to stimulate creative thinking.

24. A. I am most likely to bring charts, graphs, and printouts to a meeting so we will have some meaningful data.
    B. I am most likely to bring information about goals and deadlines to a meeting.

25. A. When confronted with a problem, I want to make the right decision based on the facts and data I can find.
    B. When confronted with a problem, I prefer to use some type of flow chart or diagram, and find an answer to the problem.

26. A. The best meetings focus on hearing what everyone has to say.
    B. The best meetings occur when you look for creative ways to get things done.

27. A. I am bothered when I see someone is not being listened to in a meeting.
    B. I am bothered during a meeting if we do not identify and prioritize the issues we are discussing.

28. A. I am willing to listen to what people have to say, whether it is in the workplace or in a meeting.
    B. We should take whatever time is necessary to get all the right information before we make a decision.

29. A. When confronted with a problem, I want to be realistic, find an answer, and get the job done.
    B. When confronted with a problem, I prefer to use some type of flow chart or diagram and find an answer to the problem.

30. A. I am most likely to bring charts, graphs, and printouts to a meeting so we will have some meaningful data.
    B. I am most likely to bring some snacks to a meeting to share with everyone.

After you have completed all 30 choices, transfer your selections to the following chart:

#	TASK	TEAM	DATA	PROCESS
1.	A☐	B☐	—	—
2.	—	—	A☐	B☐
3.	A☐	—	—	B☐
4.	—	A☐	—	B☐
5.	—	A☐	B☐	—
6.	—	—	A☐	B☐
7.	A☐	—	—	B☐
8.	—	A☐	B☐	—
9.	A☐	B☐	—	—
10.	A☐	—	B☐	—
11.	—	A☐	—	B☐
12.	A☐	—	B☐	—
13.	—	—	A☐	B☐
14.	A☐	—	B☐	
15.	A☐	B☐	—	—
16.	A☐	—	B☐	—
17.	—	—	A☐	B☐
18.	—	A☐	—	B☐
19.	A☐	—	—	B☐
20.	A☐	B☐	—	—
21.	—	A☐	B☐	—
22.	A☐	B☐	—	—
23.	A☐	—	—	B☐
24.	B☐	—	A☐	—
25.	—	—	A☐	B☐
26.	—	—	A☐	B☐
27.	—	A☐	—	B☐
28.	—	A☐	B☐	—
29.	A☐	—	—	B☐
30.	—	B☐	A☐	—

Total: _____   _____   _____   _____

            TASK   TEAM   DATA   PROCESS

Maximum score in any column is 15.

A score of 10 to 15 indicates a strong tendency to work in this style. A score of 6 to 9 indicates this may be a secondary style. A score of 5 or less indicates there is little tendency to work in this style. No score of 10 or more in any column would suggest that the respondent is highly situational in his or her style of working with other people. Two scores of 10 or above would suggest that the respondent combines traits from both of the styles that received high scores. It is important to recognize your preferred style(s) along with your secondary style(s). It is equally important to examine the styles in which you scored low. You will want to be aware of your low-score areas in order to better deal with other people who have higher scores in those areas. You can also strengthen your professional performance by asking how you might enhance your contribution to your team by adding behaviors that might be found in your low scoring areas.

STYLES OF GROUP INTERACTION

Working in a group, people often adopt one (or more) of four basic personality styles. These styles will be exhibited in how a person prepares for meetings, participates in group discussion, solves problems, communicates, handles data, and uses group process tools. The four basic styles are Task Oriented, Team Oriented, Data Oriented, and Process Oriented.

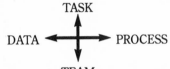

Task Orientation—The task-oriented team member focuses on getting things done. He or she is realistic, aware of deadlines, and probably sees himself or herself as pragmatic and serious-minded. Task- oriented people like to see results and may not want to spend time searching for a variety of solutions to a problem when there is a viable fix at hand.

Team Orientation—The team-oriented team member focuses on keeping the team together. He or she is interested in assuring that the team works effectively, that everyone has the chance to participate, and listens well to what people are saying. Team-oriented people are interested in results, but they want team members to achieve a consensus about what the results should be.

Data Orientation—The data oriented team member focuses on getting the right data in order to make effective decisions and plans. The data-oriented team member is often unconcerned as to whether he or she is working alone or with a team. In fact, working with a team can be a problem for data-oriented people if the team is not willing to responsibly collect and utilize data. Data-oriented team members do not want to have to spend time fixing a problem over and over again. They prefer to get the right data and fix it once.

Process Orientation—The process-oriented team member focuses on finding elegant solutions to problems and making order out of chaos. Process-oriented team members are often seen as creative and a bit unconventional. They are often interested in using visual tools, such as flow diagrams, cause-and-effect diagrams, and process mapping as tools to use individually and in group work. Process-oriented people may act as a spark plug to keep the team active, or can become bored and can disrupt the team's activities.

7

Resolving Conflicts Within Teams and Between Teams

Over time, one of the major challenges for any team is to resolve conflicts that exist within the team and between the team and other work groups. The appendix to this chapter includes a useful instrument for evaluating styles of resovling conflict.

CONFLICT IS NORMAL

Conflict within the team and with other organizations may not be pleasant, but it is perfectly normal in any work setting. We will always have situations where our interests differ from those of the people around us, and these differences cause conflict. The trick is not to avoid conflict, but to know how to effectively resolve conflict in a way that accomplishes the tasks of the team and still maintains the health of the team.

Some normal conflicts that could occur in a team include issues like who gets to take vacation when, who has to work outside in bad weather, or how to spend the money in the budget for tools. There can be many sources of conflict between your team and other groups. For example, your team may want to work on a job at a certain time, but you cannot get the parts when you want them.

The place to start in any conflict is with understanding what your interests are, and what the interests of other people may be. You want to work on getting your interests met, not on running over the opposition. The best way to resolve differences is to understand everyone's interests, talk about them, and find the best way to meet everyone's needs (Fisher, 1981).

The win-win approach to conflict resolution is a strong part of the team culture at Saturn. Saturn teams approach conflict from a "win-win or no-deal" point of view, in which the team either comes up with an answer that satisfies all parties or does not make a decision (Bolton, 1993). In some cases, teams at Saturn will elevate conflicts that they cannot resolve in a win-win manner, meaning that a middle manager must get involved to sort out the differing needs and mediate the issue or make the decision.

Getting upset with other people does almost no good. The other people are just seeking to meet their interests, so they will consider their actions to be valid because their needs are as valid as yours. You may disagree about whose needs should get priority, but people may disagree with you based on their perceptions and the expectations they have from their management.

STEPS FOR RESOLVING TEAM CONFLICTS

1. Know what your interests are and know the interests of the people you must deal with.

2. Don't get into an argument over a position that others take. Instead, understand their interests and find a way to help them meet their interests while meeting your interests too.

3. Separate the person from the problem. Focus on meeting interests. Attacking people just makes it harder to communicate and get your interests met.

4. Put yourself in the other's shoes. Discuss their perceptions.

5. Recognize your own emotions. Let the others blow off steam, if necessary, but don't react to emotional outbursts.

6. Find out where your interests and their interests are compatible.

7. Realize that each person often has multiple interests.

8. Invent new options.

9. Make it easy for them to agree with you.

10. Use objective criteria.

Having objective criteria makes it easier to resolve a conflict. If your team has data that illustrates the problem, it is easier to get other people to see things your way and help you improve the situation.

In some cases, conflicts can be resolved by resorting to a fair procedure. Work assignments, for instance, can be made by taking turns, drawing lots, or flipping a coin.

TEAM LEADER'S PERSPECTIVE

Use the ten steps for resolving conflicts as a coaching tool for your team. A team can survive conflict when there are healthy balances in the emotional bank accounts. Encourage the team to view conflict as a creative process that forces the team to come up with the best course of action.

One effective way to resolve conflict is to bring the team back to the mission. What is the team here to do? How does this conflict relate to the mission? Are their objective criteria or evidence (such as your performance indicators) that will settle the disagreement?

MIDDLE MANAGER'S PERSPECTIVE

The middle manager will need to intervene when a team is coming apart due to internal conflict. In some cases it may be necessary to separate the people who are in greatest conflict. Reassignments are sometimes the best answer.

The middle manager also must intervene in conflicts between teams that are not being effectively resolved at the team level. These often relate to lack of clarity regarding the teams' roles and responsibilities that create unmet expectations. The middle manager is the guardian of the boundaries and must settle boundary disputes.

In some cases the middle manager must make the decision to settle an issue. In these cases it is important to point out that the organization prefers to make a decision through consensus, but that when a consensus cannot be achieved and a decision must be made, it is management's responsibility to force the issue and make the call. Use these situations as a lesson for the teams. If they cannot sort it out on their own, then you will do it for them and they may not like your answer as much as one of their own making, so in the future they need to work harder to reach a quick consensus.

Effective teams can be rough on each other because the team members are emotionally committed to their mission and their team. Be careful not to punish a team for being aggressive. Instead, encourage the team to remember the importance of maintaining a healthy emotional bank account with the other teams in the organization.

APPENDIX

Assessing Styles for Resolving Conflict

This instrument is designed to give individuals feedback and information regarding how they manage conflict when working in a team environment.

INSTRUCTIONS

Please review the follow pairs of statements, thinking about them from the perspective of the team or group with which you work. For each pair, select the statement that is most like the way you feel or would respond. In some cases, neither of the choices may appeal to you, so select the one that would be most like you, considering the options. Please make your choices based on how you see yourself behaving and feeling in a group setting. Do not make your selection based on how you think you ought to act or feel, but on how you think you really would act or feel.

1. A. I need to be active in setting goals to make sure the goals meet my needs and interests.
   B. I need to work out agreements in setting goals so that other people's interests and my interests are both met.

2. A. I focus on making sure others understand my position during meetings.
   B. I am often not interested in stating my position or hearing what position other people may take during a meeting.

3. A. I should be recognized when I perform work well.
   B. The team should be recognized when we perform work well, even if my extra contribution might be overlooked.

4. A. When there is a problem to solve I prefer to team up with other good people to work on it.
   B. When there is a problem to solve, I would rather solve it my way instead of compromising with someone else.

5. A. I will take extra time to help make a decision that meets everyone's interests and needs.
   B. I will go along with a decision even if my needs are not met.

6. A. It is better to not commit to support goals you do not agree with.
   B. I tend to support the goals set by customers, co-workers, or management.

7. A. I focus on stating my interests in a meeting and understanding the interests of other people.
   B. I focus on understanding what other people need to accomplish during a meeting.

8. A. The whole team should be recognized when we work well together.
   B. If my contributions are not recognized, I would prefer for my team to not be recognized.

9. A. When there is a problem to solve I prefer to jump in and solve it on my own.
   B. When there is a problem to solve I will let others jump in and work on it first.

10. A. I need to be active in decision making to protect my interests.
    B. It is better to reach no decision at all than to reach a decision that does not meet my needs.

11. A. I need to work out agreement with others on goals.
    B. It is better to not commit to goals you do not agree with.

12. A. I need to be active in decision making to protect my interests.
    B. I will take extra time to help make a decision that will meet everyone's interests.

13. A. When there is a problem to solve, I would rather solve it my way instead of compromising with someone else.
    B. When there is a problem to solve, I will let others jump in and work on it first.

14. A. I focus on making sure others understand my position.
    B. I focus on stating my interests and understanding the interests and needs of others.

15. A. The whole team should be recognized when we work well together.
    B. The team should be recognized, even if my extra contribution might be overlooked.

16. A. I need to be active in setting goals to make sure the goals will meet my needs.

B. It is better to not commit to goals you do not agree with.

17. A. I focus on making sure others understand my position.
    B. I focus on understanding what other people need.

18. A. I should be recognized when I perform well.
    B. The whole team should be recognized when we work well together.

19. A. When there is a problem to solve, I prefer to jump in and solve it on my own.
    B. When there is a problem to solve, I would rather solve it my own way instead of compromising with someone else.

20. A. It is better to reach no decision at all than to reach a decision that does not meet my needs.
    B. I will go along with a decision even if my needs are not met.

21. A. I need to be active in setting goals to make sure the goals meet my needs.
    B. I tend to support the goals set by customers, co-workers, and my management.

22. A. I am often not interested in stating my position or hearing what position other people may take during a meeting.
    B. I focus on understanding what other people need to accomplish during a meeting.

23. A. I should be recognized when I perform well.
    B. If my contributions are not recognized, I would prefer my team not be recognized.

24. A. When there is a problem to solve, I prefer to team up with other good people to work on it.
    B. When there is a problem to solve, I will let others jump in and work on it first.

25. A. I will take extra time to help make a decision that meets everyones' interests.
    B. It is better to reach no decision at all than to reach a decision that does not meet my needs.

26. A. I prefer to work out agreements with others when setting goals.
    B. I tend to support the goals set by customers, co-workers, or my management.

27. A. I focus on stating my interests and understanding the interests of other people.
    B. I focus on understanding what other people need.

28. A. If my contributions are not recognized, I would prefer for my team to not be recognized.
    B. The team should be recognized, even if my extra contribution might be overlooked.

29. A. When there is a problem to solve, I prefer to jump in and solve it on my own.
    B. When there is a problem to solve, I prefer to team up with other good people who want to work on it.

30. A. I need to be active in decision making to protect my interests.
    B. I will go along with a decision even if my needs are not met.

After you have completed all 30 choices, transfer your selections to the following chart:

#	Win/Lose	Win/Win	Lose/Lose	Lose/Win
1.	A□	B□	—	—
2.	A□	—	B□	—
3.	A□	—	—	B□
4.	—	A□	B□	—
5.	—	A□	—	B□
6.	—	—	A□	B□
7.	—	A□	—	B□
8.	—	A□	B□	—
9.	A□	—	—	B□
10.	A□	—	B□	—
11.	—	A□	B□	—
12.	A□	B□	—	—
13.	—	—	A□	B□
14.	A□	B□	—	—
15.	—	A□	—	B□
16.	A□	—	B□	—
17.	A□	—	—	B□
18.	A□	B□	—	—
19.	A□	—	B□	—
20.	—	—	A□	B□
21.	A□	—	—	B□
22.	—	—	A□	B□
23.	A□	—	B□	—
24.	—	A□	—	B□
25.	—	A□	B□	—
26.	—	A□	—	B□
27.	—	A□	B□	—
28.	—	—	A□	B□
29.	A□	B□	—	—
30.	A□	—	—	B□

Total: _____   _____   _____   _____
       Win/Lose   Win/Win   Lose/Lose   Lose/Win

Maximum score in any column is 15.

A score of 10 to 15 indicates a strong tendency to approach conflict situations within a team in this style. A score of 6 to 10 indicates this may be a secondary approach to dealing with conflict situations in a team setting. A score of 5 or less indicates a low preference for this style. No score higher than 9 in any column indicates there is no preferred style. The individual may deal with conflict in a highly situational manner. If there are two scores above 10, look for the similarity in both high-scoring styles. For example, Win/Lose and Lose/Lose both share a common low concern for other people's needs. Win/Lose and Win/Win both share a high task orientation.

This instrument is designed to provide feedback based on your response to the forced choice selections. It is often beneficial to ask people who are members of your team for their observations and feedback to validate or expand on the feedback from this instrument. The instrument assesses the degree of focus you bring to meeting task demands and meeting the needs of other people around you. How you respond to task demands and people influences whether your approach to conflict is Win/Lose, Lose/Lose, Lose/Win, or Win/Win.

Lose-lose—The Lose-Lose style indicates a low focus on task accomplishment coupled with a low focus on addressing the needs of other people.

Win-lose—The Win-Lose style indicates a high focus on task accomplishment coupled with a low focus on addressing the needs of other people.

Lose-win—The Lose-Win style indicates a low focus on task accomplishment coupled with a high focus on addressing the needs of other people.

Win-win—The Win-Win style indicates a high focus on task accomplishment coupled with a high focus on addressing the needs of other people.

8

Running
Effective Team Meetings

Teams need to meet regularly to plan, make decisions, share information, and solve problems. Some meetings are effective and some are not. It is important to develop effective meeting habits.

THE SPHERE OF INFLUENCE

Team members need to recognize that they have a sphere of influence and a sphere of concern. Usually, the sphere of concern may be greater than the sphere of influence. Spending time on issues that are outside of the team's sphere of influence is usually not productive (Covey, 1989).

The sphere of influence includes all the things that the team can actually do something about. This includes the resources the team controls, the time of the team members, and the attitudes of the team members. Meetings that focus on what the team controls will have positive results.

The sphere of concerns includes all the things that the team may be concerned about, such as pay, overtime, getting more team members, meeting customer expectations, and the success of the overall company. Some of a team's concerns will fall within their sphere of influence. In this case, the team members will be able to effectively address these concerns, because they control the resources, time, and attitudes that can determine how a concern will be resolved. In other cases, the concerns are outside of the sphere of influence of the team. In these situations, the team has only two choices. One is to not spend any time on the concern, since it is outside the sphere of influence. The other choice is to work on expanding the team's sphere of influence to be able to influence the issue that concerns the team.

The team's sphere of influence will vary from one organization to the next. However, here are some examples of the types of activities within the sphere of influence of teams in several organizations. At Chaparral Steel, teams focus on production issues—such as backlogs and man hours required for each ton of steel produced—as well as the financial indicators of the plant, since team efforts directly impact financial performance (Dumaine, 1990). Teams at the Miller Brewing Company work nine hours per day with one hour of overtime provided for daily team meetings. The teams at Miller make shift assignments, decide on the frequency of rotating assignments, discuss safety and quality, and address productivity and work performance issues (Wellins et al., 1994). Saturn teams have a wide sphere of influence that includes waste minimization, maintenance needs, material and inventory control, record keeping, and work plans (Bolton, 1993).

MEETINGS MATRIX

There are all sorts of issues that a team might think about working on during its meetings. Some issues are urgent, others are not. Some issues are important, others are not. It is helpful to construct a meetings matrix that helps team members keep track of the issues they are working on. A helpful matrix is shown in Table 8.1.

Table 8.1
Meetings Matrix

	URGENT	NOT URGENT
IMPORTANT	**1** Crisis decisions Solving problems	**2** Appraising situations Planning Identifying potential problems Improving processes
NOT IMPORTANT	**3** Issues the team can resolve in 5 minutes Delegated Items	**4** Self-centered behaviors

To be effective, the team wants to maximize the time it spends working on quadrant two issues—things that are important, but not urgent. Maximizing the work in quadrant two helps the team stay out of quadrant one (fire fighting) by keeping the fires from getting started in the first place.

The team will need to spend some time on quadrant three issues, which are urgent, but not important. These necessary items should be worked on quickly and the team should then move on to the quadrant two issues.

The team needs to stay out of quadrant four. If team members think they are drifting into quadrant four, they should speak up and let others know that they are concerned that the team is going to have an ineffective meeting.

Sometimes the team must work on quadrant one to address a crisis or to solve a problem. Quadrant one issues can best be handled when the team members focus on having clear objectives, use rational decision making, and use data to solve problems.

EFFECTIVE MEETING HABITS

The following are the basic rules for conducting effective team meetings that become habit forming for your team(s):

1. Plan an agenda ahead of time and make sure that people know what they will be working on during the meeting.

2. Invite the people who need to attend. When you know what you will be working on you can invite the right people to be there with the right information. This might include customers or people from support organizations.

3. Maximize the time you spend working on quadrant two issues.

4. Use rational decision making to stay on track.

5. Use task actions and maintenance actions to help the group stay together and get things done. (See Chapter 9.)

6. Look for win-win outcomes.

7. Stay in your sphere of influence.

PARKING LOTS

Sometimes issues come up in a meeting that will derail the meeting, dragging the participants off onto some tangent. Some issues arise that are too volatile to be addressed immediately in a team meeting. For both of these reasons, it is effective for the team to maintain a "parking lot" where issues can be parked for future resolution. When an issue comes up that needs to be addressed, but not right at the immediate point in time, the team can agree to put the issue in the parking lot to be saved for future discussion. This allows a team to stay focused on the most important issues without losing track of other issues that need to be handled. Issues in the parking lot can be addressed at the close of the meeting, if there is time, or in a future meeting.

CREATIVE TOOLS TO PUMP UP YOUR TEAM MEETINGS

In the initial stages of forming a team, team meetings are exciting and stimulating. People are working on problems that have irritated them for a long time and breakthroughs are often abundant. Over time, the team will pick the low-hanging fruit and the improvements become harder to achieve. When teams start to reach a steady state, there are actions that can be taken to pump up the team meetings to keep them at a high energy level.

Mountain Climbing

Mountain climbing is a creative thinking tool. The objective is to generate new ideas that will help the team make performance breakthroughs. Steps in mountain climbing include the following:

1. Identify the current state and the desired future state that the team wants to achieve regarding some issue.

2. Imagine that there is a mountain between the current state and the future state. The shortest way between the current and future state will be to go over the mountain.

3. Define the traditional ideas and steps the organization would normally take to get from the current state to the future state. Define these traditional actions as the long winding road around the base of the mountain.

4. Now create paths over the mountain that are new and innovative. Strive for three levels of alpine crossings. The first level will be ideas that are a bit unusual for the organization but that are certainly possible actions. Think of how the organization has used out of the box ideas in the past. The second level will be way out-of-the-box ideas that you've heard about at other places or that you think would be highly unusual, but remotely possible. The third level goes right over the top of the mountain, through the clouds. These are the really off-the-wall ideas that might be absolutely crazy. Generate as many of these as possible. The ideas you come up with at the cloud-and-mountain peak level will stimulate ideas that you can use at lower alpine levels.

5. After you have described many paths up and over the mountain, let it rest for a while and then come back and select the path that is best for your organization.

Remember the ancient Chinese saying: Many mountains up to heaven, many pathways up each mountain.

Kinesthetic Stimulators

Many adults are kinesthetic learners. This means that they learn primarily form sensory experience. Kinesthetic learners may be uncomfortable sitting in team meetings where there is "nothing to do." Talking about issues does not stimulate their thinking and creativity.

Kinesthetic learners respond to having objects present in the meeting environment that they can manipulate to stimulate their thinking processes. Team meeting rooms should have a small set of building blocks on the table top, yo-yos, Play-Dough, and a variety of small Nerf toys and balls that can be tossed and squeezed.

While this may give an appearance that does not match the serious tone of the workplace, kinesthetic stimulators can make a great difference in a team's output. Kinesthetic thinkers will be able to channel their energy and focus on achieving team objectives.

Mind Maps

A great amount of research has gone into the study of human thinking processes. Most cognitive psychologists agree that individuals tend to utilize either the left side or the right side of their brain in thinking. Left-brain thinkers prefer to think in an orderly and rational manner, being comfortable with mathematics, logic, and thinking in sequence. Right-brain thinkers prefer to think in terms of relationships and patterns, and make more use of intuitive leaps in understanding.

Most teams in the work environment will consist of a mix of left- and right-brain thinkers. Some professions may attract people with a common thinking style, so some teams may be overloaded with people who have a common way of processing information and framing situations.

Many of the tools covered in this book are designed to stimulate left brain thinking, such as the planning and decision making tools. Other concepts, such as mountain climbing, are designed to stimulate right brain thinking.

Mind mapping is a tool designed to stimulate both the left brain and the right brain in thinking for individuals and groups (Buzan, 1989). Mind mapping is a proven tool for stimulating thinking and for improving memory. Figure 8.1 is an example of a Mind Map developed for preparing a presentation or report on improving safety.

Steps in creating a mind map include the following:

1. Start with a colored image in the center of the page.

2. Draw images throughout the mind map.

3. Print when writing.

4. Print on the lines of the mind map.

5. Use colors throughout.

6. Pull up from the team all their ideas about the central topic.

Mind maps can be used by teams to stimulate and organize their thinking about any topic. Mind maps are also useful for organizing thoughts for writing procedures, developing training, preparing presentations, and writing reports.

Figure 8.1
Mind Map Example

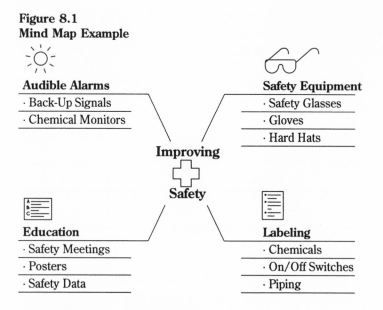

Audible Alarms   **Safety Equipment**
· Back-Up Signals   · Safety Glasses
· Chemical Monitors   · Gloves
                                             · Hard Hats

                        Improving

                          Safety

Education   **Labeling**
· Safety Meetings   · Chemicals
· Posters   · On/Off Switches
· Safety Data   · Piping

TEAM LEADER'S PERSPECTIVE

It is the team leader's duty to ensure that the team carves out time to have effective meetings. If the team does not take the time to have meetings, consensus within the group breaks down and performance indicators are not reviewed. Effective teams are constantly learning about issues and constantly improving their processes. Without team meetings, the learning and improvement cycle runs off the track.

The team leader is also responsible for making sure that the team's work is kept visible through the use of posted performance indicators and easel pads for posting the team's work where all the team members can see it. Does this mean the team leader wields the marker in the meetings? Probably not. In many cases it is a good idea to ask a team member to wield the pen for the group.

MIDDLE MANAGER'S PERSPECTIVE

The middle manager is responsible for assuring that there is an appropriate place for teams to meet. Some organizations set aside "team rooms" that are dedicated for team meetings. These rooms have the team's performance indicators posted for ready reference.

The middle manager should observe each team during a meeting and give the team leader feedback about the meeting's effectiveness at some time after the meeting. The middle manager is also responsible for assuring that the fullest possible information about the organization is being fed to the team for use in meetings. At the very least, the middle manager can hand-write a weekly information page that is copied and given to all teams to keep them informed about the organization's overall performance.

9

Maintaining the Teams

A work team, like most groups, has a life cycle. There are many ways to describe this life cycle, but in general a team goes through certain phases. These phases can occur quickly in a project team, and may take years to all occur in a work team (Knowles, 1972).

In general, teams start by going through an uncomfortable start-up phase. The start-up phase involves the team members in learning what they are to do, figuring out how they are going to work together, and getting to know each other. There is sometimes discomfort for team members during this phase, since people are uncertain about how to act and what to do. The team members need some time to sort things out and make personal decisions about their commitment to the team.

From start-up, teams often move next to a testing phase. In the testing phase, team members are testing each other, testing the boundaries of what their team can do, and testing their management to see if management is really going to let the team control the issues within their boundaries. The testing phase sometimes involves conflict within the team and conflict with people outside the team about the boundary issues.

Eventually, teams move into a performance phase, which can last for a long time. In the performance phase, the team members have learned how to work as a team, understand their mission, perform their tasks, and, in general, are comfortable working as a team. The output of teams in the performance phase is usually very high and people usually enjoy working in this setting.

Often, teams drop briefly out of the performance phase and into a temporary retesting phase when new people join the team. The addition of just one person may not cause much retesting, but if several people are added to or moved from the team, the team will naturally go back through a brief

Figure 9.1
Phase Movement in Teams

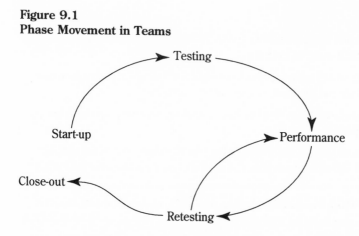

start-up and testing process to redefine roles and get everyone up to speed with each other and the team process. Changing people often means that the team will change the way it does business.

In some cases, teams end with a *close-out* phase. This is common in project teams, where the team's work is finished, so the team members wrap up their work and disband. People move on to other jobs and the team ceases to exist. When this happens, team members need to give themselves permission to feel some loss about the close-out of the team. People will miss the friendship and feeling of accomplishment they experienced when the team was working at an optimum level.

MAINTENANCE ACTIONS

We've already noted that in every team setting there are two issues that must both be worked on at the same time. One issue is to accomplish the *tasks* of the team. If the team does not deliever on its products and services to its customers, it will fail. The second issue is the *maintenance* of the team so that it does not fly apart in the process of accomplishing the tasks. Some of the actions of team members must be focused on maintaining the team so that it can function (Benne and Sheats, 1948). Typical maintenance actions include:

- *Encouraging* each other to contribute ideas and to keep pushing on the tough-to-resolve issues.

- *Resolving* differences of opinion so that the team keeps a win/win approach to getting things done.

- *Gate keeping,* which means keeping everyone involved. We act as a gate keeper when we notice that someone has not said much lately and we ask him or her to participate.

- *Humor* is a maintenance action that defuses tension.

TASK ACTIONS

Other actions of team members focus on helping the team accomplish its tasks. Typical task actions include:

- *Scanning,* in which team members determine the range of issues they need to address and put their issues into a proper priority.

- *Establishing objectives,* so that the team members agree on what they are out to accomplish.

- *Collecting data,* so that the team can have an objective criteria for making decisions. This includes seeking data and sharing data and information with others.

- *Decision making,* using data to decide what to do to accomplish the team's objectives. This includes each team member being willing and able to express his or her opinions.

- *Process improvement,* studying how processes work and figuring out how to improve the process to be more effective.

- *Planning,* to define who is going to do what and when.

- *Summarizing,* to review what the team has covered in a meeting and what it has decided to do.

SELF-CENTERED BEHAVIOR

Some actions of team members do not contribute to the team's accomplishment of tasks and may tax the maintenance of the team. Instead of helping the team to function, some team members may contribute to the dysfunction of the group. Dysfunctional actions include:

- *Diverting* the team by going off on tangents or raising issues that are unrelated to the team's current issues.

- *Blocking* the team by refusing to accept a reasonable win/win course of action.

- *Attacking* other team members for their personalities, background, or ideas.

- *Dominating* the group by taking up all the air time and not allowing others to contribute their ideas or observations.

- *Withdrawing* from the group by not attending team meetings or by not participating in team discussions.

REFLECTING ON HOW THE TEAM WORKS

There are many ways to improve the performance of teams. One way is to invest some time during team meetings to talk about how the team is working. This discussion can help team members assess where they are in the life cycle of the team, and it can make it possible for team members to talk about their performance strengths and weaknesses in a positive way (Marsick, 1990).

One effective way for the team to diagnose itself is through the use of a metaphor for discussion. This is often done effectively by identifying a sports metaphor that helps people discuss their team's performance in a nonthreatening way. From a creative thinking perspective, reflective practice stimulates right-brain thinking in a group in a manner that opens the group up for new insights about their performance.

Reflective practice is a concept pioneered among adult educators to create new learning about life situations. As a learning tool, reflective practice involves people in critiquing the presuppositions on which their beliefs about a situation have been built (Mezirow, 1990). Educators employ a variety of tools to stimulate reflective thinking, such as group discussion, structured interviewing techniques, role playing, and workshops. For example, Victoria Marsick, at Columbia University, has documented reflective practice workshops taught at the Management Institute, Lund, Sweden, in which participants work on team projects and critique their participation and challenge one another's thinking to gain self-insight (Marsick, 1990).

A reflective practice team-building session brings participants together and starts by using exercises and ideas that help people "get out of the box" to create new revelations about how the team functions on a daily basis. Lockheed Martin's sessions have employed a sports metaphor to encourage participants to look at their current behaviors from a very different perspective.

A LOOK AT SPORTS

The world of professional sports is very different from the everyday work world for most employees. Professional athletes are paid very high salaries for performing in a very public manner. Coaches prepare the athletes to perform using a disciplined set of specialized skills. This type of guidance rarely exists in the workplace.

However, there are many good reasons to use a sports metaphor to open up dialogue and discussion within the organization. First, most organizations can correspond their work to a particular sporting event. Second, many people are sports enthusiasts and will relate to a sports metaphor once they understand how it connects to their work. Third, the use of a sports metaphor encourages creative thinking in the organization as people use the metaphor to redefine their working relationships. Fourth, the sports metaphor is a nonthreatening (and fun) way to look at the organization. Using this kind of open dialogue allows some tough truths to surface in a healthy manner.

There are obvious similarities between work and sports. Both activities involve rules or boundaries that must be observed. Team sports, like work, requires an understanding of who will do what and when. Team sports and the workplace both have a roster of "players" who exercise certain skills as well as "others," such as owners, referees, the media, and the spectators, who also have a stake in the performance outcome. The sports team's performance is recorded and analyzed for improvement opportunities, just as the performance of work teams can be recorded and analyzed for continuous improvement.

PLANNING A REFLECTIVE PRACTICE SESSION

Most organized activities that are designed to improve the function of a group fall under the category of "team building." Unfortunately, when people talk about having a "team building session," many odd images are conjured up. Surely it must be time to stoke up the fires, spread out hot coals for the group to walk on, and perform the tribal dance! However, many forms of "team building" that effectively engender trust and understanding within a work group do exist.

The event planners first determine what sports metaphor really fits their organization. For example, most factory environments can identify with the football metaphor, with the production group as their offensive line and the human resources, environmental, and health and safety groups on the defensive line. Staff organizations, on the other hand, tend to correlate with the basketball metaphor. In staff groups, the ball is often moved around to set up a successful play. In our large corporate structures, people in similar positions can identify with the metaphor of playing golf. In this environment, the course is the same for everyone, but the individuals understand that it is their individual skill that will show progress.

The facilitators work with their managerial clients to select the right sports metaphor and then consult with management to determine who should attend the team building session. Questions to be addressed by the team building leaders include:

- What and why is there a need for this reflective practice session?

- Who are the key players on the team for the purpose of this session?

- Can this session be scheduled on a date and time that is acceptable to all the key participants? (Note: this is a must, because if one person is missing, the session will not be as effective.)

- Where should this team building session be held? Do we need an environment away from the workforce, or does that pose a problem? (Note: the author recommends getting away from the office.)

The team building facilitators next prepare a thorough list of discussion questions designed to capture the group's imagination and keep them stimulated. The team building leaders should fully explore the selected sports metaphor to capitalize on facilitating discussion points. The discussion questions must not be given to participants prior to the session. When facilitating, the team-building leaders need to remember to discuss only one question at a time.

Special arrangements are usually made to foster a sense of teamwork. A small token (such as a golf tee, a wiffle ball, or a sponge football) representing the theme of the meeting and presented by the team building leader will serve as a reminder of the team building event for participants.

HIKE THE BALL

The football metaphor works well to stimulate reflective thinking in factories and production-related organizations since they are similar to a football team in their function. They have an offensive line, such as the actual production group, maintenance, planning and scheduling, and marketing, as well as a defensive line which includes human resources, health & safety, and environmental protection.

To conduct a team building session around the football metaphor, the facilitator gathers the key managers together and asks them to define the similarities between their organization and a football team. The facilitator is prepared with a series of questions that will get the process rolling.

1. How is our organization similar to a football team?

2. If we are like a football team, what position does each of us play? Who plays offense and who plays defense? Do we have any special teams? Who is the quarterback? Does everyone really know what position he is supposed to play?

The facilitator then uses other prepared questions that will encourage the participants to discuss the real issues of the organization within the metaphor of football.

3. If our business were a football team, what would be our own version of clipping? Of intentional downing? Of unsportsman like conduct? Of holding? Of face masking?

4. If our business were a football team, let's consider the "game film." What are three examples of excellent plays we have run that achieved major yardage or a touchdown?

5. What are three examples of plays where we have been thrown for a loss, fumbled the ball, or suffered interceptions? Why did they occur and what will we do to keep that from happening next time?

As reflective practice, the football metaphor encourages people to talk about issues that may not be easily discussed, but they are approached from the perspective that to win, we must examine how we are running our plays. The review of the game film encourages the team members to express positive observations about the group that have often gone unstated. This process also provides an important opportunity for critical evaluation of the group's performance and encourages the participants to confront their problems in a caring manner in which everyone is committed to making the team a success.

THE TIP-OFF

The basketball metaphor has worked well to stimulate reflective thinking in staff organizations. Staff groups function like a basketball team in that staff members have to coordinate their work to be successful. Staff groups often work at a constant running pace that is close to a basketball pace, and staff members often must know how to perform each others' duties to function smoothly.

Again, the facilitator starts by asking the participants to identify the similarities between their jobs and the game of basketball, allowing them to elaborate on the similarities as much as possible. This is followed by the same types of questions as in the football exercise that will allow the group to discuss the types of penalties that can occur that harm teamwork and a review of the best and worst plays that the team has recently experienced.

The author has used the basketball metaphor with staff groups in the human resources field with excellent results. Staff team members were encouraged to discuss how they move the ball around to score, the fast pace of the game, penalties, and fouls. The staff participants enjoyed the opportunity to identify examples of where they really played well as a team and developed their own list of attributes of high-performance teamwork. They also critiqued situations when their teamwork was insufficient and developed ideas that will keep their team focused on effective teamwork.

The basketall metaphor also relates well to health care settings where doctors, nurses, and technicians all "pass the ball" around to meet the needs of the patient.

FORE

The golf metaphor stimulates reflective thinking in branch staff groups in large organizations such as public relations. Branch organizations are compared to golf because they have the same course of action (or work) and use individualized skills to accomplish their mission.

To conduct a team building session around the golf metaphor, the facilitator prepares a series of questions that will encourage discussion.

1. What is the course in our organization? Are there similarities or differences between the various organizations within the corporation?

2. If our organization functions like a golf team, what obstacles have kept us from completing the course? What is our version of a sandtrap, rough, and water obstacles?

3. What do we need in our individual golf bags? Examples could be cellular phones, pagers, facsimile machines, and so forth.

4. What events in the organization correspond to "pars," "birdies," and "holes-in-one?" How can the team members better publicize these successes when they occur?

5. What can we do as team members that will turn a bogie into a score of par or better?

6. How can we become more of a team, rather than individual players within the corporate structure?

Again, this reflective practice using the golf metaphor invites open discussion to encourage participants to team with other corporate professionals. Reflective practice brings out potential solutions to problems and can enhance communications and a corporate image.

TRACK AND FIELD

Quality professionals often find themselves working together in the same quality organization, but specialized in functions such as auditing, corrective actions, or total quality management. Teamwork and communication between these functional areas may be low and stress builds up regarding how these functions work, or do not work, together.

Teamwork among quality professionals and other similar groups can be improved by employing a reflective practice session built around a track-and- field metaphor. In track and field, each individual may compete (or work) as an individual, often in a specialized capacity. The overall success of the team, however, depends on the sum score of all the individuals. If the team is weak in one area, the overall perception of the team by their customers in the line organization is diminished.

The track-and-field metaphor has given quality professionals a new and interesting way to look at how they work together, and to address issues from the sports world that pertain to their work, such as being in proper condition, achieving a "personal best," and having confidence that someone else on your team is not about to put a javelin in your back.

COACH'S CORNER

The following coaching points are based on experiences in Lockheed Martin:

1. Not everyone in the reflective practice exercise will know the sport you are using as a metaphor. Make sure that a diagram is provided for everyone that outlines the key positions of the sport and rules of the game, to "level the playing field."

2. A few people will really resonate with the idea right away. Let them take the ball and run with it, then bring the rest of the group along by asking specific people to add their thoughts.

3. Humor goes a long way. If you are using the football metaphor, cue up a "bloopers" tape that shows some amusing plays. Movie rental stores usually have a wide range of comical sports videos to use for this purpose.

4. Supplement the session with some serious videos that support the sports metaphor. Try using the Lou Holtz tape *Do Right* to reinforce the football metaphor.

5. The object of a team building session is for the participants to answer the questions, not the team building leaders. Collect all thoughts on an easel pad and display it throughout the room.

6. It is extremely important to stay focused and be patient. The team will not succeed when the group is fragmented. Combine the team's thoughts into a workable solution for all, but remember to let the ideas flow.

WHY USE REFLECTIVE PRACTICE?

Why should your organization use reflective practice methods and what can you expect to achieve from this tool?

First, people in organizations often become complacent about issues in their culture that are unhealthy or dysfunctional. People may have become lax about reporting problems or may be reluctant to offer suggestions for improvement. There may be systemic problems with the manner in which people communicate, or confusion over the roles that people are expected to play. The reflective practice exercises that employ sports as a metaphor give people a safe opportunity to surface the issues that need to be discussed.

Reflective practice creates a sudden, and often unexpected, opportunity for people to express their feelings about issues that often go unaddressed. Instead of denying that problems exist, concerns are safely brought to the surface and can be addressed within the established framework of the sports metaphor. Reviewing the "game footage" requires everyone to acknowledge both the strengths and the weaknesses of the team and offers an opportunity for people to pull together.

Several goals can be achieved from conducting a reflective practice session.

1. Participants will identify the examples of where they have worked well as a team. The attributes of effective teamwork will be defined by the team mem-

bers based on their own behaviors and experiences.

2. Situations where team effort has been less than perfect will be reviewed in a supportive setting. By comparing the good team experiences with the problems that the team has encountered, people can identify the changes in communication, expectation, and support that are necessary to operate as a successful team all the time.

3. The sports metaphor will clarify role expectations and clear the air about any confusion that may have existed concerning who is to do what. The interrelationships of team members are improved by discussing who plays what role on the team.

4. Reflective practice helps to drive fear out of the organization. Fear is reduced when people can talk about their concerns in a caring setting that reinforces the need to work together for common success.

CONCLUSIONS ABOUT MAINTAINING THE TEAM

Effective team building often comes from opening up channels of communication and encouraging people to share their experiences of wins and losses, joys, and frustrations. Most people have difficulty opening up and sharing their thoughts, particularly when it means discussing things that hurt, like performance problems, unmet expectations, and dissatisfied customers.

TEAM LEADER'S PERSPECTIVE

The team leader must keep his or her finger on the pulse of the team. The team leader assesses whether or not the team is accomplshing its tasks and the degree to which the team is maintaining itself. This requires a careful balance over time. The team leader can critique the team on task performance and suggest new tools and methods to improve task work. The team leader can also recommend team-building activities to sustain the team.

MIDDLE MANAGER'S PERSPECTIVE

The middle manager must observe the task performance of the teams and assure that work is being done. The middle manager must not hesitate to confront a team when the task expectations are not being met, but must ask the team to come up with the changes they will make to stay on task. Middle managers must provide time and resources to support team maintenance activities. This means approving an occastional day off for team building and finding funds to provide a meal to celebrate a team's milestones and accomplishments.

10

Process Improvement
and Teams

One of the key responsibilities of a team is to take ownership of its work processes and seek to improve those processes. There are lots of ways to improve the work process. Before a team jumps in with ideas for upgrading equipment and adding computers, it is usually a good idea to spend some time studying what is already in place. This is often referred to as looking at your "as is" process and then figuring out how to improve it.

There are many reasons why people avoid improving their process. First, it takes time. Some people are working with processes that are so inefficient and ineffective that they must work as fast as they can all the time just to stay caught up with their work, so they will claim they are too busy to improve. Others avoid improving because it means acknowledging that the process is not really effective and they are embarrassed to admit it (Juran, 1964).

ALL WORK IS A PROCESS

Any kind of work is a process that has inputs, some type of transformation, and outputs. The outputs are the products and services that the customers receive. Of course, what the inputs and outputs are depends on what type of work is being done.

Each team will have a unique set of processes that it works with, and a unique set of inputs and outputs. The team members need to recognize these and take responsibility for improving them. Teams can often just make a list of the processes they use. Brainstorming a list of processes often generates plenty of opportunities for the team to start making improvements. In some cases it helps for the team to develop an input-process-output model to define processes.

The input-process-output model is a classic tool for helping teams assess their processes. The team starts by defining its outputs: the products or services it delivers. The team then identifies the inputs it receives to do its work. Inputs could include materials, information, procedures, power, and facilities. The team then identifies the processes it uses to turn the inputs into some type of useful work that provides the outputs to customers.

Select one of the team's major processes and identify what are the inputs to the process, the components of the process, and the outputs. Inputs could include materials you receive from other groups or vendors, and it could include information or data that you use. The process components could include the equipment and tools you use, the knowledge you apply, and the people who work on the process. The outputs are the products and services for customers as well as the waste that your process might generate (Figure 10.1).

Figure 10.1
Process Input/Output

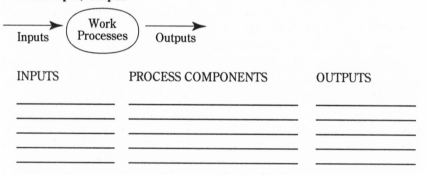

The process can be improved by working on the inputs, working on the process components, or reducing the waste or scrap that is included in your outputs.

IDENTIFY THE PROCESS FLOW

It is important for the team to identify the existing flow of work in the as is process. This is done by constructing a flow diagram that illustrates the steps and sequence in the work.

Flow diagrams allow us to visually define how a work process is performed. With a flow diagram you can show how the work is done in its proper sequence of steps. Flow diagrams provide team members with common reference points and a standard language to use when talking about an existing process.

Flow diagrams can be used to define problems, to identify which steps are adding value and which steps are only adding cost, to show interfaces between organizations where communications might break down, and to determine places where it would be useful to collect data and use control charts.

Flow diagrams allow us to identify where bottlenecks may be restraining the flow of work in a process and where we may have excess work capacity that is not effectively adding value to the organization.

In a flow diagram, some steps in the process are actions that are taken. These actions are shown in a box.

Other steps are decisions that must be made. Decisions are shown in a diamond.

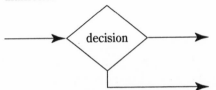

The steps in the diagram are connected to show the sequence in which each step occurs. Lines with arrows are used to connect the boxes and diamonds so we can see the flow of the process.

For example, when a team conducts a focus group session with customers, they follow a process that can be shown through a flow diagram (Figure 10.2).

Figure 10.2
Flow Diagram

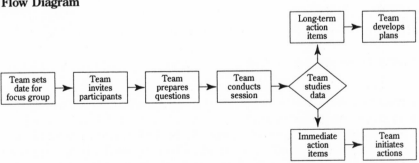

Start by identifying all the steps in the process and drawing them in a diagram. You can then work to reduce the cycle time, reduce scrap, eliminate rework, eliminate non-value-adding activities, and redesign the work so that it is more effective and easier to do.

CYCLE TIME

Cycle time is the length of time that it takes for work to run through all the steps you have identified in the flow diagram. In some flow diagrams the work cycle time may be minutes. In others, it may be months. In most cases, shortening the cycle time means reducing the cost of the work and making the work easier to perform. You can shorten the cycle time in several ways.

1. Find the bottleneck resources. These are the steps that constrain the speed of the entire process. The bottleneck is the step that is the slowest step in the whole process. The whole process will not work any faster than the bottleneck does.

2. Look at the sequence of the steps. Sometimes you can improve cycle time by changing the order in which the work is conducted.

WORK THE BOTTLENECKS

The bottleneck resources define the overall rate of work in any process. If, for example, there is only one person available to take samples on a given shift and the request for samples far outruns the amount of work the sampler can perform, the sampling becomes a bottleneck that constrains the entire work process. Finding a creative way to conduct more sampling would speed up the overall process.

REDUCE SCRAP AND REWORK

The greatest improvement in the efficiency of a process often comes from finding out how to reduce scrap and re-work. Work that produces scrap is work that has wasted time, materials, and the capability of the process to produce good products and services. To reduce scrap and rework the team members need to collect data about what type of scrap and rework is in their process. The team needs to use the data and their knowledge of the work process to figure out how to reduce the scrap.

Rework will often jump out at you once you construct the flow diagram. You can see the places where work must be evaluated and sent back to be done again if it is not right. Those are the places to focus your attention to reduce scrap and rework.

Time spent on rework adds no value to the team. The only steps that add value are the steps that lead directly to providing a product or service to the customer. Non-value-adding steps only add cost to the product or service. An effective team will keep looking for ways to eliminate the non-value-adding steps.

EXCESS CAPACITY

Sometimes the team can become more effective by doing less work. If your output is controlled by the rate of output of your bottleneck resources, why spend time and money fully operating nonbottleneck resources? To do so only generates excess materials that must be stored until the bottlenecks can be worked through. Having to store excess materials adds to the cost of your process by requiring space to store this excess inventory (Goldratt and Cox, 1984).

SURVEYS

In many cases an improvement effort may require more information from customers or people who are doing the work. There are several ways to seek people's opinions or thoughts about a situation. One approach is to conduct a focus group session. A cross-section, or a subsection of the organization may be gathered together in a conference room. A facilitator will pose a question to the group, such as "what do you see as problems or opportunities for our organization?" The group brainstorms their views and opinions, which the facilitator records on an easel. An overall list of concerns or ideas is then prepared, without identifying who offered specific thoughts. Focus groups can be used with teams or with representatives from a group of teams. They can also be used by teams and managers who are seeking input from customers or other groups.

Teams sometimes seek to improve a process by developing and administering a survey. Surveys can be useful tools for collecting data if several basic guidelines are followed.

They can include several types of questions. Some are factual, like "what is your age?" Some are opinion based, like "what do you think about this product?" Some are open-ended and require an in-depth response; others are close-ended, requiring a specific response such as yes or no.

Several effective formats can be used to design surveys. Surveys can use a "put the check in a box" approach in which respondents check off their answers. Other surveys employ a rating method in which respondents are asked to indicate whether they strongly agree, agree, disagree, or strongly disagree with a proposal or issue. Card sorts are another effective tool in which people sort through a deck of cards that have statements on them. The respondents arrange the cards in order of preference.

When a survey is being designed, it is important to avoid several possible biases in construction. Avoid using emotional words, such as "deadbeat," which will bias the respondent. Avoid using leading questions. Avoid using questions that create anxiety. Clear instructions should be included with questions that are not self-explanatory. In most cases it is important to include a cover letter that goes along with a survey. The cover letter needs to tell people why the survey is important and how to return the survey, and should clarify how respondees will be identified, or whether they will remain anonymous.

CHECK SHEETS AND DATA COLLECTION

Data can be collected in many ways to assist in improvement of a team's work processes. Methods such as check sheets, logbooks, surveys, and questionnaires are common forms of data collection. Check sheets allow people to record information about what is happening in their daily work as events occur. To set up a check sheet, the team should decide what events it will be recording and what time frame to use for collecting data. Table 10.1 shows a sample check sheet.

Table 10.1
Check Sheet for Phone Calls at Work

Calls for William	√√√
Calls for Sharon	√√√√
Calls for Mike	√√√√ √√√√ √√
Calls for Rose	√√√√ √
Calls for Eddie	√√

Some basic guidelines for collecting data are:

1. Consider the purpose for collecting the data and then collect the appropriate data.

2. The data you collect must be related to your source population.

3. Proper interpretation of data often requires that the data be tested for statistical significance.

4. Keep your use of data honest! Don't weed out the information that disagrees with the team's hypothesis.

5. Let people know what is going on. If you ask people to collect data without letting them know why they are doing it, they may become apprehensive about how the data will be used.

6. People must never be punished for what the data reveal. If you punish people, they may not accurately report the data in the future.

DATA MATRIXES

The data matrix is a powerful tool for helping teams diagnose their work performance and the overall health of a work system. This tool is prepared by developing a chart that compares data by looking at issues such as performance over time. The matrix enables the team to break complicated data into a readily understandable format. Table 10.2 shows a sample data matrix.

Table 10.2:
Matrix of People and Time of Events

Number of Errors Found by Inspectors

	April	May	June	July	August	Total
Bill	3	2	1	2	2	10
Sue	0	1	1	0	1	3
Gail	4	5	9	3	4	25
Alex	1	3	0	0	0	4
TOTAL	8	11	11	5	7	42

In the example shown in Table 10.2 the data matrix allows us to review the work of several people over several months. Review of the data shows that there were a larger number of errors in May and June. We note that Gail tends to find more errors than the other inspectors, especially compared to Sue and Alex.

The data matrix can be used to compare a wide range of performance activities, including types of defects over time, types of customer complaints over time, and defect rates from one machine or product line compared to others over time.

THE PARETO DIAGRAM

The Pareto diagram (Figure 10.3) is a tool that allows teams to arrange

Figure 10.3
Pareto Diagram

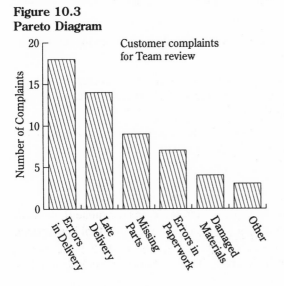

data to compare the relative significance of events or costs. The diagram is named after the Italian economist Vilfredo Pareto. There are five common steps to preparing a Pareto diagram:

1. Decide which data should be on the chart.

2. Decide on the time period for which the data will be collected.

3. Collect the data on a worksheet (e.g., from budgets, cost reports, and other sources).

4. Construct the Pareto diagram from the data collected. Arrange the data cells in descending order from the left of the graph.

5. Add information to make the chart readable to other people.

HISTOGRAMS

The histogram (Figure 10.4) is a bar graph that provides a snapshot of the pattern of variation in the process the team is studying. Decide which characteristic will be targeted for data collection and then select the width of the cells to be used for displaying the data. Select the cell width in a way that best displays the data so that it is neither too vague nor too busy. A good histogram needs about sixty values or measurements.

Figure 10.4
Histogram

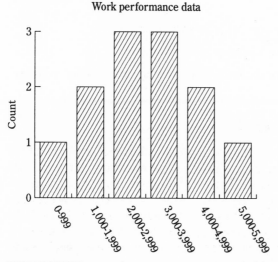

Work performance data

RUN CHARTS

A run chart (Figure 10.5) is a line graph that displays data without any statistical control limits. It can be useful for teams in analyzing data in the developmental stage of a product or prior to establishing a state of statistical control.

To create a run chart, begin by establishing the vertical scale as the quality characteristic the team is measuring, such as viscosity, temperature, pH level, decibels, weight, or distance. Use the horizontal scale to show time intervals, sample numbers, or order of production. It is important that the data be shown in the proper sequence of when events occurred.

Figure 10.5
Run Chart

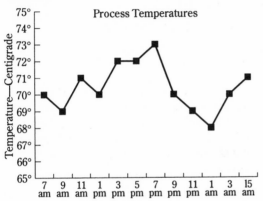

You can establish whether or not there is a trend in the run chart data by looking for situations such as:

1. Eight points in a row above or below the median line.

2. Six consecutively rising or six consecutively falling points.

3. The points show a pattern of change over equal time intervals that indicates "periodicity" of data.

STATISTICAL CONTROL CHARTS

Control charts are tools that help teams understand the variation in their work processes. Without an understanding of process variation, teams can get caught trying to fix problems that are inherent in the work system.

Variation that is inherent in the work system is referred to as common cause variation. This variation comes from the equipment that is used, the materials that are used, and the approved procedures for performing work.

Other variations are introduced into the work system when people adjust equipment, buy a new brand of material, change an operator, or revise a procedure. This is referred to as special cause variation.

For example, a baseball pitcher might normally throw a ball in a range of 92 to 98 miles per hour. This variation is built into his system and is therefore common cause variation. But if the pitcher has a bad headache one day, his average pitch may drop to 88 miles per hour. This variation is not part of the normal performance system and is special cause variation.

Control charts help people visualize the pattern of variation in a process and determine whether the variation is built into the system or is due to special causes. Control charts deal with two types of data: attributes and variables.

Attributes data are counting data: the number of bad eggs in a dozen or the number of scratches on a new automobile. There is no such thing as half a bad egg or half a scratch. It is either there or not there.

Variables data consist of measurements on a continuous scale: today's temperature, miles per hour, or the time it takes to mow a lawn. Different types of control charts are used for tracking attributes and variables data.

If a team decides to use control charts to track variation, it is essential to employ a degreed statistician to help design the control charts. There are too many subtle aspects of control charting to turn a team loose to create their own.

SEARCHING FOR THE ROOT CAUSE

Sometimes problems arise with a system that are tough to fix. We take action but the solution we try does not really fix the problem. Often this is due to not understanding what the root cause of the problem is and not addressing the root cause. When a root cause is not addressed, then most of the attempts to fix the symptoms of the problem will not be effective. Many team efforts make extensive use of root cause analysis (see Chapter 11) as a way to drive continuous improvement. Union Carbide's teams at their Texas City plant, for example, routinely employ root cause analysis as an effective tool for figuring out how to fix a problem the first time so that it stays fixed (Bauman, 1993).

PROCESS IMPROVEMENT AS A COMMON TEAM ACTIVITY

Process improvement is one of the most widely cited activities of cross-functional teams and cohesive work teams. This activity provides relief to the team members by eliminating problems and hassles in their work and provides cost savings and elimination of regulatory problems for organizations.

For example, a team of laboratory personnel at SwedishAmerican Hospital conducted an improvement study of arterial blood gas tests. Using flow diagrams and cycle time reduction, the team was able to make significant breakthroughs to reduce the cost of the analytical process (French and Hermansen, 1997). These types of case examples are legion in the quality literature and have been the driving force for formation of teams in many organizations.

TEAM LEADER'S PERSPECTIVE

The team leader's role is to keep the team organized and focused on improving the work process. In most teams there is an abundance of ideas for removing bottlenecks and eliminating scrap and rework. The team leader needs to capture the ideas and provide the rigor that makes sure that action plans are developed to work all the issues and that follow-up attention is given to improvement efforts. Lots of meetings will generate good ideas that fail to materialize unless the team leader has good minutes and the responsibility for following up on actions is clearly established.

The team leader plays an important role outside the team meeting in following up on process improvement ideas and encouraging team members to work the issues. An effective team leader will coach and help team members in getting things done. This way, when the team gets back together for a meeting, there will not be a big letdown because no one has taken any action. The team leader artfully pushes team members so that there will be successes to report back to the whole team.

MIDDLE MANAGER'S PERSPECTIVE

The middle manager plays a vital role in the teams' process improvement efforts. It is up to the middle manager to find out what resources the teams need to achieve improvements and then get the resources for the teams. Middle managers are "bilingual," speaking both the language of the workplace (machines, products, customers) and the language of the senior management (money) (Juran, 1964). Therefore, the middle managers take the teams' ideas and find ways to express the improvements in financial terms to get the resources the teams require.

The middle managers will also be champions for the teams in getting the "rocks" out of the road. Rocks in the road may be poor training, poor procedures, or ineffective company policies. These are conditions that the teams suffer under and often do not have the authority or resources to fix on their own. Enter the middle manager, who will find ways to fix these system problems. When middle managers spend some of their time sitting in on team meetings, they are aware of the types of problems the teams are encountering and can determine what types of actions need to be taken to smooth out the road for the teams.

11

In Search of the Root Cause

For effective long-term process improvement, teams need to be able to identify and address the root cause of problems that cause errors. Managers in a team environment must make root cause analysis one of their primary interests since it is management's role to get the rocks out of the road for the teams.

WHAT TYPES OF PROBLEMS NEED ROOT CAUSE ANALYSIS?

An operator in a steam plant shuts off a critical valve, which causes a system to malfunction, leading to a million-dollar plant shut down. The pilot of an oil tanker fails to turn his vessel at the proper time, causing the ship to run aground and spill its cargo. The cockpit crew of an airliner does not realize their wing flaps are not properly set before take off, leading to a tragic loss of life.

All of these might sound like topics for the evening news, and in every case there would be an investigation into the cause of the incident. Some people would study the situation to find out what actually happened. Others might be primarily concerned with who to blame for the problem and who is going to be liable for the damages. A few might even suggest that we should find out the root cause of the incident to assure that it does not happen again. What may not be clear in any of these approaches is what we are really trying to learn, because the language of root cause analysis and problem solving is often misunderstood.

DEFINING A PROBLEM

The first difficulty is to agree on what we mean when we say that we have a problem. For instance, I might say I have a problem regarding how I am going to get up on my roof to clean the leaves out of my gutter. I might have a more serious problem of explaining to my wife why I am not going to clean the leaves out of the gutter, but am going to go camping this weekend instead. In some cases we use the word "problem" when we are describing a tough decision we have to make, or when we have to develop a plan of action. We call these problems because they are sometimes difficult things for us to do.

For the purpose of root cause analysis, a problem is a situation where the performance of some system does not meet the performance you expect to have. For instance, you might expect your washing machine to run through all its cycles, but instead you find that it frequently goes out of balance in the spin-dry setting. Or, you might purchase a new home computer and find that the system will not work in the manner you were expecting. In both of these cases we have a situation where the expected performance does not match the real performance, so we have a problem.

FINDING THE IMMEDIATE CAUSE

When you have a problem it is important to first identify the immediate cause. The immediate cause will be the action, or series of actions, that directly creates the difference between expected and real performance.

In some cases the immediate cause will be simple and openly visible. A valve on a water system is left open, and the operator of the system freely admits that he mistakenly left the valve open, so we know the immediate cause of the problem. Or there is an automobile accident and the blood alcohol level of the driver who crossed the center line shows he was heavily intoxicated.

In other cases, the immediate cause of a problem may be hidden and may take some investigative work. In an airplane accident, there may not be an obvious cause of the crash. The investigators will need to use a questioning process to help them gather the important facts about the accident before they begin to develop theories of possible cause. Effective questioning will seek to define the problem and narrow the scope of possible causes by describing what the problem is, where it exists, when it happened, and whether the problem is increasing in scope, staying the same, or going away. One of the best questioning methodologies for identifying the immediate cause of a problem was developed by Kepner and Tregoe through their research on how scientists ask questions to solve problems (Kepner and Tregoe, 1981).

ACTIONS TO BE TAKEN

Once we know the immediate cause of a problem we are often in a position where we must choose an action to take. Actions related to problems often provide a short-term, temporary solution, which may be inexpensive and which only requires us to know the immediate cause of the problem. Other actions may require us to find the root cause of the problem so we can take permanent, corrective action.

Around the house we may be tempted to opt for a short-term fix with the problematic washing machine, by placing a block of wood under one side to tilt the machine so that it no longer stops during the spin-dry cycle. When we choose this type of solution, we congratulate ourselves for finding a creative solution and for not having to pay a repairman to work on the problem.

These same thoughts might likewise seduce us to opt for the short-term fix with a problem in the work environment. For example, there may be a need to repair some copper tubing that supplies coolant to a motor. Proper procedure may require that an engineer be contacted, and that we diagnose the reason for the tubing to have failed in the first place. However, in the interest of saving money, saving time, and cutting through organizational red tape, one might have the local maintenance crew take care of the job when they have some extra time, and not even bother logging the work as having been performed. After all, it saved money, and everyone who needs to know about the repair work was present when the decision was made to take this short cut. We pat ourselves on the back, just as we would at home.

The short-term fix is very seductive to many organizations. However, in the long term, these quick fixes can create many new problems, and may cause us to fail to see significant inadequacies in our operating processes.

The most seductive part of the short-term fix is that by choosing the short-term option, we only need to know the immediate cause of the problem. This means we do not have to extend our questioning into the search for the root cause. This is a reward for us, since looking for root cause often means asking embarrassing questions about how the organization functions. The longer an organization goes without asking these tough questions, the more ingrained the systemic problems will become.

LOOKING FOR THE ROOT CAUSE

The root cause is the most basic causal factor, or factors, which, if corrected or removed, will prevent the recurrence of the situation. Root causes create the setting for the immediate causes of the problems.

The search for root cause consists of a questioning process. Several tools can help us structure our questioning, and we shall look at how these tools might be used. However, it is important to understand where one looks for root causes that create the setting for the immediate causes of our problems. Roots are found in the soil, and the soil of organizations is referred to as the systemic factors that deal with how the management of the organization plans, organizes, controls, and provides assurance of quality and safety in six key areas: personnel, procedures, design, material, training, and management.

Because root cause analysis means asking difficult and sometimes embarrassing questions about how we choose to manage our organizations, it is a questioning process that might be left undone for internal political reasons. Janis has conducted extensive research on the way in which people in an organization will reinforce their own beliefs and behaviors through mutual rationalization (Janis, 1972). Any effort to question these insulated views of reality will be considered an assault by a hostile force. The questioner will be subject to both indirect and direct pressure to not rock the boat.

TOOLS FOR QUESTIONING

Teams or individuals can use four basic tools for structuring the questioning process. The first tool is a structured questioning process known as questioning to the void. The second tool is a process diagram to visually display the sequence of events. The third tool describes the problem in terms of protective barriers that have failed. The fourth tool seeks to focus on changes that have occurred relative to the expected and real performance of a process. Other tools, such as fault tree analysis, are best used by the safety and quality specialists who can participate in extensive training to correctly use these approaches.

Questioning to the Void

In essence, all root cause analysis is a questioning process. Different tools provide different ways to structure the questions and the information. Questioning to the void is a quick, conceptual tool that focuses people on the root cause.

Questioning to the void means continuing to ask the same basic question, over and over again, until you have identified the systemic issue in which the root cause resides. There are many variations of the same basic question: What caused this? Why is this so? When, why, or how did this come about?

The main requirements for questioning to the void are bulldog tenacity, a willingness to ask embarrassing questions, and an understanding of systemic issues so you will know when you have arrived at a root cause.

As Figure 11.1 shows, questioning to the void is a convergent thinking process where the questioning leads to a more and more narrow set of possibilities.

The Process Diagram

The process diagram seeks to establish the chronological sequence of

Figure 11.1
Convergent Thinking Process

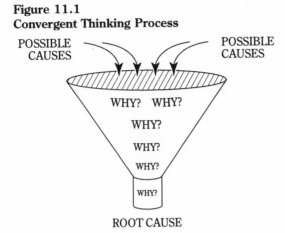

POSSIBLE CAUSES

POSSIBLE CAUSES

WHY? WHY?

WHY?

WHY?

WHY?

WHY?

ROOT CAUSE

thoughts and events leading up to the problem. Each action or thought will be placed in a box, linked together in a line, leading to the accident or malfunction. Once the relevant events have all been identified and placed in their proper sequence, the investigator will look at each step or action and ask, "What allowed this to happen?" The conditions that allowed the specific actions to occur will be diagrammed as circles or ovals above or below the event on the chart, and will be connected to the appropriate event with a line. The diagram provides a visual tool for imaging all the actions relevant to the problem, and for visually tracing the actions back to their roots among the systemic issues of the organization. Figure 11.2 what the basic process diagram will look like.

Figure 11.2
Process Diagram

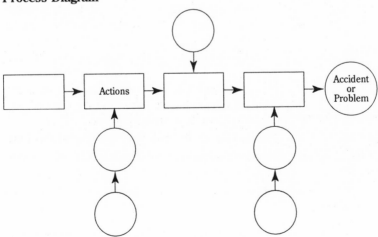

Actions

Accident or Problem

The process diagram allows us to visually see the display of the events leading to the problem and the factors that allowed the events to exist.

BARRIER ANALYSIS

Barrier analysis provides a structured way to envision the events related to a failure of a system or the creation of a problem. In barrier analysis we seek to identify the barriers and controls that will remove or reduce hazards, enforce compliance with procedures, or make "targets" invulnerable to hazards. Figure 11.3 illustrates analysis of the source of a problem. The target or victim of the situation, and barriers that are supposed to be in place

Figure 11.3
Barrier Analysis

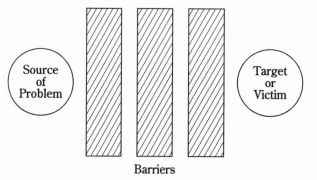

Barriers

to protect the target from the source of the problem.

One example of a barrier analysis might be to consider the problems related to an oil tanker accident. The source of the potential problem would be the crude oil being shipped in the tanker. The potential target, or victim, would be the marine life and shorelines in the area affected by a spill.

A number of possible barriers might keep the oil from encountering the marine life or minimize the impact of a spill. These barriers might include design barriers, training and qualification barriers, and containment and clean-up procedures and equipment.

An oil tanker may be designed with a double hull to prevent rupture of the vessel, and the oil within a tanker can be stored in a number of small internal holds. If the tanker is designed with a single hull and a small number of large holds, the tanker will be more efficient in passage, but ineffective as a barrier against an environmental insult.

The crew of a tanker may be required to be staffed at a certain level, and there may be qualifications required for crew members before they are allowed to handle certain valves or to navigate in certain waters. Likewise, there may be requirements regarding control of substance abuse aboard the tanker. However, if understaffed crews are allowed to operate the ships, and if underqualified people pilot the tankers, and if there are systemic substance abuse problems among the crew, then there will be no effective barrier against collision or grounding of the vessel.

Even if an oil tanker runs aground and begins to spill its cargo, there may be a barrier in the containment and clean-up equipment that can be strategically located to minimize the damage. However, if the equipment is not available, or if the operators are not well trained, the clean-up operation may be an inadequate barrier to protect the victim from the oil spill.

Barriers may be physical requirements, procedural actions, or installed assurance activities. An organization can impose administrative controls and verification controls upon itself that serve as barriers against potential problems.

For instance, to ensure the quality of a design, an organization may require that it be independently reviewed by another qualified engineer, separate from the original designer.

An organization may place stringent controls on how it will handle drawings, and on how the drawings will be numbered, stored, and used in the field. There may be well defined steps regarding how changes to drawings will be made, and how controlled drawings will be provided to the people who use the drawings.

Training is another form of assurance activity. In all industries it is important that the operators and maintenance people be properly trained, and that the organization have evidence of the proper design, delivery, and completion of the training programs. The assurance of the training is often as important as the training itself.

However, when using the barrier analysis to determine what object or assurance activity either failed or was missing from the process that led to the immediate cause of the problem, it is important to keep asking questions. It is vital to discover why a critical barrier was left out or why the management system allowed inadequacies in barriers to exist. Knowing which barrier was faulty does not explain why it was faulty, and that is an embarrassing question which needs to be asked.

Change Analysis

A fourth basic tool for conducting a root cause analysis is referred to as change analysis. In change analysis the questioner seeks to compare the present state of the system (which is the real, nonfunctioning situation) with the prior state in which the system worked properly. The object is to identify what has changed in the system between the time in which the system worked and the time that it failed. Changes then will be investigated to determine whether they had a significant effect.

However, change analysis must be followed by additional questioning to determine how the changes were permitted to occur. It is always important to continue the questioning process into the arena of the systemic factors.

SYSTEMIC FACTORS

Systemic factors concern how the management of the organization plans, organizes, controls, and provides assurance of quality in five key areas: personnel, procedures, equipment, material, and the environment. These five areas constitute the total work system. Each area can be broken into several parts.

The personnel systemic factors (Figure 11.4) include issues of internal communication, training, and human factors such as physical health, mental health, substance abuse, and mental attention. If an organization involves people in technical tasks but has no way of ensuring they are functionally literate, it is setting itself up for major problems. If training is casual, not rigorously planned and executed, employees may have significant gaps in their knowledge of how to do their work. Training should include both general familiar ization with the overall organization and specific performance-based instruction to master work tasks. The organization must also consider how it deals with other human factors. For instance, are employees required to work extensive overtime, and, if so, what effect does this have on safety and quality? How does the organization ensure that substance abuse and other personal problems are identified and counseling and rehabilitation are available?

Figure 11.4
Personnel Systemic Factors

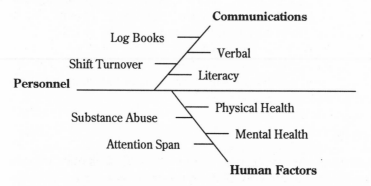

The procedural systemic factors (Figure 11.5) concern how the organization chooses to develop and handle procedures to establish how the work should be done. Are the procedures clearly written? Are they reviewed for accuracy by someone other than the person who wrote them? Are they up to date? Are they available to the people performing the work?

Figure 11.5
Procedural Systemic Factors

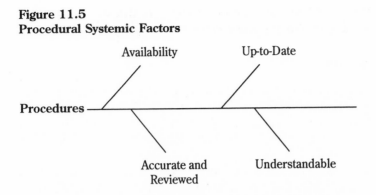

The equipment systemic factors (Figure 11.6) address how equipment is designed, selected, operated, and maintained. Has the organization selected the proper type of equipment for a task? Was the equipment properly designed, manufactured, and installed? Was the equipment periodically maintained? Are there surveillance systems in place to ensure that proper maintenance is performed? Were the operators trained to use the equipment? Are the operators using statistical control limits to measure their work, or are they making adjustments as they see fit?

Figure 11.6
Equipment Systemic Factors

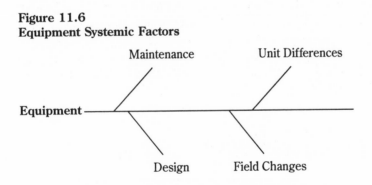

The materials systemic issues (Figure 11.7) relate to how the process's raw materials are being used. How do you specify which materials should be purchased? How does the organization ensure that the materials meet specifications? Does the organization require evidence of statistical control from its suppliers? Does the organization rely on on-site inspection of the suppliers' facilities, or does it inspect suppliers' products before use? Once an organization receives materials, how does it ensure they are properly used? Does the organization have a system for controlling the identification of materials to ensure they do not get mixed up and misused? When materials are stored, how does the organization ensure they do not become lost or damaged? The same questions about incoming materials for use in a process also apply to the end product of your organization. How do you ensure its quality and protect it during storage and shipping?

Figure 11.7
Materials Systemic Factors

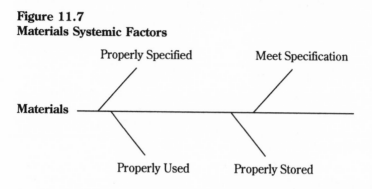

The environmental systemic issues (Figure 11.8) involve how to handle natural and man-made environmental conditions in the work area. How does the organization protect its people, equipment, and materials from adverse environmental factors such as rain, snow, extreme temperatures, and humidity? How does the organization protect its people, equipment, and materials from man-made hazards such as radiation, corrosive gases and liquids, high temperatures, and explosive conditions? What systematic methods are in place to deal with these hazards? Environmental issues also include the system an organization has in place to deal with the by-products of its primary manufacturing system. How does the organization control air contaminants, hazardous chemicals, toxic substances, dangerous fumes, and radioactive waste?

Figure 11.8
Environmental Systemic Factors

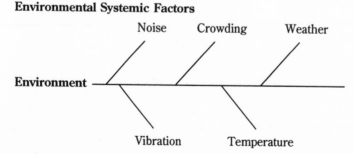

ASKING EMBARRASSING QUESTIONS

How do you know when you are on the right track with your root cause analysis? You are probably on the right track when you are asking embarrassing questions that people in the organization normally do not discuss.

How far should we go in pursuing the root cause? You have certainly gone too far when you start discussing theology! The root cause will be in the soil of the organization, which consists of the systemic issues of how we choose to manage the resources of our business, governmental, health care, and nonprofit organizations.

TEAM LEADER'S PERSPECTIVE

The team leader needs to keep a watchful eye for problems that recur or that the team does not seem to be able to fix. In some cases this will indicate that there is a root cause that must be addressed before the problem will truly go away.

MIDDLE MANAGER'S PERSPECTIVE

Root cause analysis is a primary function of middle management. The middle manager is in a position to see a broad set of problems in the organization and can ask the difficult questions necessary to find the root cause. Since root causes are found in the organization's systems, and since management creates the systems, it is management's role and responsibility to identify the root causes of problems embedded in the systems and to fix them for the benefit of the teams, the customers, and the entire organization.

12

Cross-Functional Teams

WORKING ACROSS ORGANIZATIONAL BOUNDARIES

Many work processes require diagnosis and remedial actions that demand cooperation across traditional organizational boundaries. In some cases, organizations reengineer the organization to remove the boundaries and to redesign the work. In other cases, organizations form special cross-functional teams, with members from all the impacted work groups, who will work together to improve a process or solve a problem.

Cross-functional teams are special types of teams that require a different set of ground rules to be successful. The cross-functional teams are sometimes ineffective because of the barriers generated due to organizational politics.

The cross-functional team is often the first serious application of team technology for many organizations. Many companies, such as Xerox, have made the extensive use of cross-functional teams the cornerstone of their quality programs that are credited with saving the company (Palmero and Watson, 1993). Lockheed Martin began the extensive use of cross-functional teams in its heritage companies in the late 1970s. The commentary on cross-functional teams in this chapter is drawn from observation of teams within Lockheed Martin as these teams gradually gained acceptance as an effective way of doing business.

The cross-functional team is a formally chartered group of people who are given permission to embark upon a quest within their company. This idea has been around for a long time, but it was Joseph Juran who gave the concept new life in his recommendations for creating "cross-boundary" project teams to tackle specific improvement opportunities (Juran, 1964).

For organizations to effectively implement cross-functional teams, several issues must be resolved. These include how the teams will function within the organization, who will sponsor the teams, who will facilitate the team effort, who the team participants will be, and how the team will report its recommendations.

BEHIND THE CASTLE WALLS

When we strip away the façades, many corporations resemble a medieval landscape. The company may function as if it exists on an island where new ideas are kept far across the sea. On the island there may be many castles, each with its own royalty, knights, and serfs. A worker must swear an oath of fealty to his or her castle and must be wary of appearing too friendly with the lords of other manors if he wishes to get along in the castle. Of course, the Earl of Manufacturing may find it difficult to cooperate with the Princess of Procurement. But from behind their fortress walls, the realm appears to be an orderly place to live.

Across the land there are dragons. Some are native to the island (common-cause dragons), and some fly in for seasonal foraging (special-cause dragons). Woe unto the unfortunate serf or knight who brings bad tidings of a dragon, for while these dragons may plague the kingdom, the king or queen may be offended to hear of this pestilence.

EMBARKING ON A QUEST

When the ravages of the dragons become too great to ignore, the nobility may deem it proper to commission a party to embark on a quest to rid the realm of the offending beasts. The makeup of this quest (the cross-functional team) is of crucial importance. The team must include representatives from each of the castles whose lands the dragons have defiled. If, for example, the castle of the dwarf king has a stake in the outcome, but no fighting dwarfs are included in the quest, then the recommendations from the whole team may be rejected out-of-hand by the dwarf lord.

THE ROLE OF THE SPONSOR

Even more important than the inclusion of the dwarfs is the matter of securing a sponsor. Quests are not free, even though the end results may offer a dragon's horde of wealth, which will repay the investment many times over. Before the team can embark, it must have a sponsor. Just as Queen Isabella provided the financial backing for Columbus' expeditions, some member of the royalty must provide backing for the intrepid adventurers.

Part of the sponsor's role may be to provide legitimacy to the quest itself. In case the team is waylaid by a band of wood elves, the questors will be wise to have a friend in high places who can provide the party with credentials to ensure safe passage.

The sponsor may also provide advice about the makeup of the team and important information about the nature of the dragon. Further, the sponsor may be able to provide the team with the perspective of those who reside in the high towers, which is often useful to a team recruited from the court-yards and stables.

Finally, the sponsor can give the team seasoned advice about courtly eti-quette to ensure that the recommendations are presented in a manner that does not offend royal ears.

THE SERVICE OF A WIZARD

Teams can often benefit from the service of a wizard. Wizards provide special knowledge and skills to the team. A well-trained wizard can cast a variety of helpful spells and incantations, such as magic control charts, flam-ing flow diagrams, force-field analysis, and charms for group decision mak-ing. A lesser wizard will only know a few spells and will seek to cast them even when they are clearly of no practical use.

The lords and ladies of the manor must decide whether they wish to retain the use of an in-house wizard or make use of the wandering sort. There are pros and cons in either case (which is certainly an intentional pun!). The resident wizard may know the lay of the land but may also be reluctant to give up the comforts of the castle. The wandering wizard may be more objective in his or her advice or may simply be in search of some gold.

At any rate, the quality business has found a whole host of new wizards in recent years who are anxious to try out their incantations on someone. Good wizards know lots of spells, have gained wisdom through experience, and have a tendency to tell the truth, even when the truth hurts.

FUNCTIONING AS A TEAM

The team goes forth to track the dragons. Their journey, as Juran point-ed out, is first to diagnose the situation. They must study the habits of the monsters and create new knowledge about the potential for improving the situation. The diagnostic journey is followed by the remedial journey, in which the team prepares a plan for ridding the kingdom of the dragons. All along the journeys, the team must work together. The wizard can provide special knowledge, but each representative from the castles—whether serf from the field, stable, or kitchen or knight—must add his or her knowledge or perspective of the kingdom to develop an effective solution to the situa-tion.

REPORTING TO THE THRONE

With a plan of action in place, the team will report back to the crowned heads regarding how the dragons are to be slain. In some cases, the team is empowered to slay dragons with no further approval. In other cases, the commitment to action may require considerable consultation among the royal barons and countesses. In either case, the team will eventually report back. At this stage, the sponsor's advice may assist the team in preparing its presentation. Furthermore, the sponsor must be willing to vocally support the team's proposals or actions.

With any luck at all, the brave warriors will be well rewarded for their services, and life will return to normal around the island, at least until the next dragon hatches. If a team of dragon slayers has performed poorly, the members may be consigned to cleaning the stables. When a team performs well, the members may hope some day to be knighted and even find themselves seated at the table, secure within the fortress walls.

LIVING HAPPILY EVER AFTER?

If an organization does resemble the medieval countryside, then cross-functional teams may be the best vehicles around for creating change. However, one may profit by reflecting on the eventual fate of kings and castles once the people discover that they really can slay their own dragons.

SUMMARIZING THE RULES OF ENGAGEMENT

To summarize this metaphor, there are certain rules of engagement that an organization must establish to effectively organize and utilize cross-functional teams. These are

1. The team must include representatives of each organization that has a stake in the outcome.

2. The team needs a member of senior management to serve as a sponsor who will advise the team and offer technical and political wisdom.

3. The team needs a neutral person to facilitate the team. The facilitator should have a wide knowledge of group process and diagnostic tools.

4. The team needs a charter from management that defines the boundaries of their work. If they are expected to implement changes on their own, without reporting back to management, then that should be defined in the charter.

5. The team must collect data to define the as-is situation and design a plan that will lead to an improved future state.

6. The team reports its recommendations to management, or implements changes, depending on its charter.

7. The organization should recognize the efforts of the team.

TEAM LEADER'S PERSPECTIVE

The team leader should be on the lookout for problems that require a major cross-functional team effort to improve a sytem. For major problems that may require a good amount of time and expertise from many parts of the organization, the best action a team leader can take will be to advocate formation of a cross-functional team.

MIDDLE MANAGER'S PERSPECTIVE

The middle manager is often the sponsor of a cross-functional team or the management advocate of creating these teams. Middle managers are wise to make a list of the most serious problems in their organization and then to charter cross-functional teams to attack those major problem areas.

13

Continuous Learning in a Team Environment

Some things are certain in life. You can count on death, taxes, and the assurance that during the course of your life, some things are going to change. The people who make it their livelihood to study the future have suggested that the rate of change in technology is occurring at an ever increasing pace. This means that many things are going to change at work and that we each have to acquire knowledge and stay current with information that enables us to add value to our organization.

Most teams will have to deal with several issues that relate to learning, including the following:

1. What knowledge and skills do we need to have right now to do our work effectively as a team?

2. Are we staying current with the knowledge and skills we need?

3. How should we equip ourselves to be able to keep learning what we will need to know in the future?

TAKING CHARGE OF LEARNING

Management is responsible for assuring that teams have the tools they need to effectively do their jobs. This includes not only the material tools, but the knowledge tools as well. Research into the success factors in companies that have won the coveted Malcolm Baldrige National Quality Award shows a consistent pattern of investment in knowledge by winning organizations (Nadkarni, 1995). Ongoing training and education is a key success factor for every Baldrige winner.

However, team members have to take ownership of this issue and work to make sure they have what they need if they want to be successful. It is easy to act like a victim and say that you cannot do some new work because you never got the training. It's also easy to act like a victim and miss required training requalification sessions because no one told you to go.

The responsible thing to do is to develop a training plan for the team and for the team members to be responsible for meeting the plan. It becomes management's responsibility to work with the team to make sure the training is made available for the team members. If it is not, the team needs to express their concern (Adams and Hansen, 1987).

WHAT KIND OF LEARNING IS NEEDED?

Effective teams require education and training in a variety of areas. First, team members need the right technical training to perform their tasks safely and efficiently. A training matrix can be prepared to assure that all team members have the proper technical training.

Team members also need to learn about the business. Middle managers should drop in on team members and "open the books" for the team members so they are aware of how the business is performing. When team members understand the customer's perspective and the bottom-line situation, they can do a great deal to make a difference for the organization.

Team members also need developmental learning that helps maintain the team. This can occur in team building, in individual self-study, or in formal workshops that teach problem solving, quality improvement, and creative thinking methods. Team member can profit from workshops on behavioral change that can be brought into the organization from colleges and consulting firms.

Wainwright Industries, a 1994 Baldrige Award winner, provides a good example of the diversity of educational needs that an organization may want to meet for its teams (Landes, 1995). Wainwright provides training in statistical process control, communication skills, interpersonal skills, technical training, and basic skills such as math and reading.

DEVELOPING A TRAINING MATRIX

Each team needs to prepare its own unique training matrix (Table 13.1). The matrix lists what training is needed and who needs it. It might also show if there is a date by which the training must be completed to keep a certification. The matrix needs to be posted where the team has its regular meetings and needs to be updated on a timely basis.

Hopefully, training will remain a quadrant two issue (important, not urgent) for the team. The team should be able to look ahead and determine what training and education will be useful for them in the long run, and take charge of planning to assure that the team gets the training.

Table 13.1
Team Training Matrix

	Sam	Alice	Lee	Juan	Janet
OSHA refresher	2/13	3/27	4/14	4/16	7/29
First aid training	9/11				9/11
Quality tools		6/22		6/22	
Welding certification			8/16		
Budgeting workshop		10/21			

APPROACHES TO LEARNING

It is important for the manager in a team environment to be aware that there are many methods by which adults can learn. On the one hand, learning can consist of a carefully planned structure, which analyzes tasks, identifies training needs, creates lesson plans, and evaluates learning through a written or performance measurement. This is the classic form of training that is designed to close any gaps in a worker's knowledge about performing a job. In other situations, adults might work individually to define their own learning objectives and to individually collect resources and do their own studying. Another possible learning situation is for people who are working together to define their learning needs and to work together to discover what they need to know.

Each of these learning methods-the structured training, the self- directed learning, and the group-directed learning-may provide people with the knowledge they need to work effectively in a team.

The structured training model has the benefit of being very systematic. A typical structured training model would guide the person who is developing the training through several steps, including the following (Watson, 1979):

1. Diagnose problems to determine training's role.

2. Define goals and objectives.

3. Select instructional methods.

4. Plan a favorable learning climate.

5. Preselect evaluation criteria.

The structured training model is usually the preferred approach to defining technical training needs and assuring that participants in training have actually acquired a skill or knowledge. The structure model can be used by an instructional designer to prepare training materials for individuals and classes. It can also be used by teams that want to work together to define their training needs.

Not all situations for learning will fit neatly into a structured training model. In some cases learning requires involving people in group discussions and group research regarding how they will resolve issues. It can be argued that all of the process improvement activities covered in Chapter 10, for example, are actually learning processes in which the team creates new knowledge about its work processes.

This type of participatory learning is often referred to as a situation approach to learning (Lindeman, 1926). The situation approach generally involves these steps:

1. Recognition of what constitutes a situation;

2. Analysis of the situation into its constituent problems;

3. Discussion of these problems in light of available and needed experiences and information;

4. Utilization of available information and experiences for purposes of:

   a. Formulating experimental solutions;

   b. Acting upon experiment propositions with a view of testing and if necessary revamping the assumptions which discussion has revealed.

As team members diagnose their work processes, discuss their performance indicators, and discuss the linkage between their team's performance and the overall health of the organization, new learning will definitely occur. This is an educational process known as conscientization, in which people become more critically self-aware of their knowledge, their actions, and the relationship between what they know and what they do (Freire, 1985). Conscientization results in the empowerment of the individual and the team when they fully recognize and accept their role and responsibility in influencing the fate and direction of the organization.

In typical learning situations we can expect to see a learning curve that graphically illustrates the manner in which an individual learns over time. Figure 13.1 provides an example of the typical learning curve that one

Figure 13.1
Learning Curve

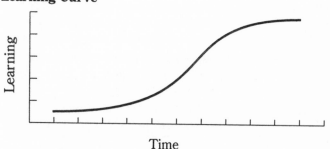

Time

might encounter in learning a technical topic, such as drafting.

However, when people are learning new concepts that engage them in conscientization, there may be a false learning peak. People learn to mouth the words about teamwork and quality, but they have not internalized the meaning of the concepts and behaviors. This is why a great deal of training about teams does not seem to take hold among managers. There is a superficial level of understanding, but understanding has not really progressed to a full state of conscientization. (I am indebted to Peter Scholtes for this observation that he made at a conference many years ago.) Figure 13.2 illustrates the false learning peak that occurs and that misleads people into superficially believing they understand team concepts. The individual must work through this false peak and come to the realization that he or she really did not fully grasp the reality of the power and synergetic force of teams, and then move on to progressing up the learning curve. Once a person has moved beyond the false peak and moves up the learning curve, examples of the benefit and need for teams become abundantly clear.

Figure 13.2
Learning Curve for Conscientization

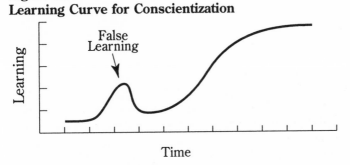

BUILDING PARTNERSHIPS

Many organizations provide for the educational needs of teams by partnering with local community colleges and universities. This partnership allows companies to provide a wide range of classes and faculty for the teams without having to invest directly in salaries and classrooms. National Semiconductor, for example, partners with the Massachusetts Institute of Technology to provide continuing education for its employees (Rau, 1995). Some companies partner with outside consultants and colleges to establish internal universities as well.

BUILDING A TEAM LIBRARY

In many cases it is useful for the team to develop its own library. A good team library includes technical resources that aid people in the technical aspects of their work as well as resources that help in managing as a team. The recommended resources would include:

- *The 7 Habits of Highly Effective People* by Stephen R. Covey
- *Quality, Cost, and Competitive Position* by W. Edwards Deming
- *Getting to Yes* by Roger Fisher and William Ury
- *The Goal* by Eliyahu M. Goldratt and Jeff Cox
- *Managerial Breakthrough* by Joseph Juran
- *The Team Handbook* by Peter R. Scholtes
- *Productive Workplaces* by Marvin Weisbord

Having a team library pays off in a lot of ways. First, you've got your own references to use when you run into difficulties and you need to consult a technical or nontechnical resource. Second, team members can borrow the materials for home study. Third, having a common set of reading material can help the team build a common understanding about how to become an effective team.

TEAM LEADER'S PERSPECTIVE

On the one hand, time spent in learning new skills and knowledge is time away from the job, so things don't get done. On the other hand, as employees become more knowledgeable, they become more valuable to the team and the entire organization. The team leader has to lead the team in deciding how to handle the issue of training so that tasks are performed and people can grow. In some cases, the team leader will champion the task issues, demanding that task accomplishment not be sacrificed for developmental purposes. In other cases, the team leader will need to insist on training and development so that the team can become more effective. This is highly situational. Above all, the team leader needs to be aware that learning is an important component in the team's success, from both a task and a maintenance perspective.

MIDDLE MANAGER'S PERSPECTIVE

Middle managers often have the most to gain by investing team resources in training. Training will make the teams more effective, which is an immediate payoff for management. Training often leads to fewer errors, lower costs, and improved employee morale, as well. However, for the middle manager, the pay-off in team training is the development of knowledgeable people who can grow into other roles in the organization. Not all teams have the right mix of people, and sometimes good people move on to other organizations and leave a gap. Investing in training is the best way to fully develop the internal resources to fill the gaps and to ensure smooth operations.

14

Creating Team Leaders

This chapter focuses on the educational process that enables the traditional supervisor to become an empowering team leader. Encouraging leaders to move from autocratic to participative leadership styles is the key to creating empowerment and a must for creating a team environment. The tough question is how to accomplish this change in leadership behavior.

If you are a senior manager or a training manager tasked with helping your supervisors' transition to leading teams, this chapter will outline the educational process you need to adopt.

FACILITATING CHANGE

Supervisors are thought to resist empowerment and to cling to autocratic behaviors because they fear loss of influence or loss of a familiar career path, and they have doubts that an empowered team will really work. Several conditions must be created in a learning setting to help leaders shift from traditional to team behaviors.

First, there must be an opportunity for supervisors to reflect on the structure of their organization, their role as leaders, and the data that has been collected over many decades on leadership styles.

Second, there must be a time for building skills that are essential to democratic leadership. People need a safe place to practice using new behavioral skills. They need time to see for themselves that they can achieve more through the use of teams.

Third, there must be a specific plan for change that prevents comfortable autocrats from avoiding the reflective-thinking and skill-building process.

Finally, there should be a coach to observe and follow up on the change process with each supervisor.

REFLECTING ON LEADERSHIP ROLES

Most supervisors are aware of problems that occur every day and are warning signs that autocratic leadership works poorly. However, the warnings are filtered out because they do not fit accepted beliefs about how a supervisor should behave. These beliefs, after all, were acquired over time, reinforced, and nurtured.

The process of learning a new leadership role begins by thinking reflectively to challenge established beliefs about what constitutes effective leadership. Reflective thinking can be encouraged by asking supervisors to draw a picture of what their organization looks like. In this nonthreatening exercise, people allow their unfettered observations to slip out and are often surprised at the pictures they create.

For example, one group of supervisors involved in this activity pictured their employees as a column of ants marching toward a hill. Supervision was seen as a cloud raining on the parade. Another group of supervisors drew a picture of employees running for their lives from a tornado labeled "upper management." On the other hand, a group of people in an empowered team doing this same exercise drew their team as people in a boat rescuing their customers who were in the water around them.

The point of this activity is to allow the images that people have about their organization to come out in a new way. This gives people an opportunity to reflect on beliefs about their organization that they may not have been ready to openly discuss.

ROLE PLAYING

Supervisors often learn a great deal from taking part in role play that allows them to experience the problems associated with working under autocratic leadership. Many organizations use role play that requires supervisors to work together to make some product like a paper airplane or a Frisbee from a paper plate. Productivity under autocratic leadership, which controls information and discourages creativity, is compared with productivity in an empowered setting.

Role playing allows supervisors to discover for themselves the disadvantages associated with autocratic leadership. Self-discovery of the problems of autocracy provides a much more profound experience than hearing about it in a lecture or videotape.

A LITTLE DOSE OF RESEARCH DATA

After supervisors have had a chance to do some self-discovery and reflect on how their behavior restricts the productivity of their organization, it's time for a bit of theory.

Most people are surprised to learn that Kurt Lewin proposed a model for democratic leadership in 1945. The four styles of leadership identified by Bradford and Lippitt in 1945 are also valid for the 1990s. Many people are surprised to learn that Tannenbaum and Schmidt published their continuum of leadership styles in the 1950s.

In addition, there are extensive studies about significant increases in productivity due to empowerment during both world wars, along with the Harwood studies, and Likert's research published in 1961.

All of this research data leads supervisors to an embarrassing question. If we've known about the benefits of democratic leadership and empowered teams for eight decades, why have we done so little to implement these ideas? That is a profound question.

PROVIDE A MODEL

Giving supervisors a model for describing the various styles of leadership helps tremendously. The problem is, which model should you use? Why not make up your own that combines several theories? Figure 14.1 illustrates a model that combines elements of Lewin, Bradford and Lippitt, Tannenbaum and Schmidt, and even a few original ideas. This model shows a continuum from hard-boiled autocratic behavior over to fully participative (or team) leadership. Along the continuum will be seen the benevolent autocrat and the consultative leader who asks for input and then makes decisions (Dew, 1997a).

Figure 14.1
Leadership Styles

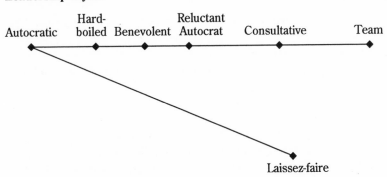

What about the "reluctant autocrat" in this model? That describes the leader who would like to be more team-oriented but does not think it would be accepted by management or the workers. Also, watch out for taking the downward slide into letting people run free by abdicating leadership responsibility and becoming a laissez-faire leader, as Kurt Lewin warned.

READY TO LEARN NEW SKILLS

When traditional leaders have had the opportunity to reflect on their situation and consider some evidence to realign their thinking, they are ripe for acquiring new team leadership behaviors. Learning new behaviors requires careful preparation in a somewhat structured learning environment.

The big question is, what behaviors constitute those needed for team leadership? A review of several surveys and case studies offers the following skills that supervisors need to master to effectively practice team leadership:

- the ability to lead participative team meetings,
- listening skills,
- the ability to handle conflict,
- the knowledge needed to establish measures,
- group centered decision-making skills,
- teaching skills, and
- team building skills.

These are skills that have been incorporated into team leadership training sessions at team-oriented facilities within Lockheed Martin.

LEADING TEAM MEETINGS

Team leaders need to gather the team together for regular meetings. The meeting is necessary for the team to study data, make decisions, identify problems, make plans, and learn about issues.

It is the team leader's responsibility to assure that an agenda is developed and that the team spends some time on its performance measures. The team leader tracks issues from the last meeting for follow-up and highlights urgent issues for immediate resolution. The team leader assures that once a decision is reached, someone accepts responsibility for implementation.

Team leaders make sure there is a regular time for the meeting and minimize interruptions. The team leader assures that there are tools, such as flipcharts, and works on achieving 100 percent attendance at the meetings. Responsibility for running the meeting might rotate from person to person.

LEARNING TO LISTEN

Effective leaders have strong listening skills in order to understand situations, improve cooperation, and encourage people to take responsibility. This is especially important in the team environment.

"Active listening," as defined by Carl Rogers, causes the listener to try to grasp the facts and the feelings of what is being communicated. The listener reflects both facts and feelings back to the speaker to assure that correct communication has occurred (Rogers, 1961).

The goal of listening is to be able to respond to the speaker's needs, not our own. We should keep listening even when the speaker's ideas and actions are different from our own. A good listener will respond with empathy, withhold judgment, and pay attention to nonverbal cues, the expression of emotion through gestures, facial expressions, breathing, posture, and tone of voice.

Supervisors need an opportunity to practice active listening by working in small groups to practice reflecting the facts and feelings being shared by others. They need to practice responding to peoples' feelings about issues, noting all the cues, and testing for understanding.

MANAGING CONFLICT

Autocratic behavior may have been an effective way for supervisors to avoid conflict with their employees. When employees are conditioned to be submissive some conflict will be avoided. On the other hand, autocracy creates resentment and leads to smoldering resistance and conflict over control. (See Chapter Seven.)

Team leaders must understand that conflict is a normal part of any team effort. Each individual has a different type of personality, different knowledge, and different experiences. It is perfectly normal for people to be in conflict. Supervisors need an opportunity to learn a bit of conflict theory and learn about their own style of handling conflict. Several good conflict style instruments are available to help people learn how they typically deal with conflict. This self-awareness allows people to perform better in conflict situations that normally arise in an organization.

Team leadership allows conflicts over issues and personalities to be resolved instead of denied. Conflict over control tends to disappear.

ESTABLISHING MEASURES

Operating in a work environment without a set of performance measures is like driving a car without a speedometer or a gas gauge. It's no wonder that organizations sometimes get into trouble under those circumstances.

A team leader will involve the people in the team in identifying what activities should be measured by the team. Establishing a good set of measures is like pitching a pup tent. There are two sides to be staked down. One side consists of the measures that are important to the customer. The other side involves measures that are important to the team. A team needs a few key measures to indicate how internal performance is going and a few to illustrate the customer's point of view. (See Chapter Three.)

Of course, the performance indicators need to be posted in a place where everyone on the team can see them. Indicators should be one of the topics in the regular team meeting. Having indicators that people cannot see is like putting the speedometer in the back seat.

GROUP DECISION MAKING

While it is certainly easier for one person to make some decisions, the quality of the decision making is often improved by involving the team. Implementation of decisions is almost always easier if everyone had an opportunity to share in the decision making. A basic truism of human behavior is that those who create tend to support.

Team leaders need to know how to guide the team in rational decision making. The objectives to be accomplished by the decision need to be agreed upon by everyone before considering the various alternatives. Even when a decision is made, the whole group should pause to identify the things that could go wrong with the decision.

In some cases team leaders will need to know how to lead a team in brainstorming and then in some form of voting. Some teams use colored dots that are placed beside brainstorming ideas. Others use a method for voting by placing weighted scores by ideas as in nominal group technique. There are many methods that work. The new team leader needs to know at least one of them. (See Chapter Five.)

In general, group decision making should be done on a consensus basis, which means that all team members can live with at least 70 percent of what is agreed upon at any time. Teams should avoid enacting decisions that give individual members significant heartburn.

TEACHING SKILLS

Team leaders do not need the teaching skills associated with non-participative learning. There is no need for lecturing or pouring knowledge into someone's head. Instead, team leaders need to awaken to the realization that we are all learning every day. When a team decides to improve a situation, it embarks on what Juran called the diagnostic journey, which is a learning process. The famed Deming Cycle was advanced by the educator John Dewey over seventy years ago as a fundamental approach to learning about the world around us. Educators call it action research because it involves the learner in taking actions in the world in which the learner lives.

The teaching skills for action research are skills related to facilitating group learning. These skills include the ability to pose questions in a manner that encourages creative thinking, the ability to guide a team in collecting data, the ability to encourage dialogue, and the knack for synthesizing ideas.

Team leaders quickly appreciate the strong link between education and participation. All learning influences the political realities of our environment, and the political environment influences all learning. Therefore, a knowledgeable work force is ready to be empowered and needs empowerment to remain vital. A work force without knowledge needs education before empowerment. Of course, the best way to prevent empowerment is to deny education, just as the best way to oppress a people is to deny them schools, literacy, and access to information that can set them free.

The opposite condition of empowerment in today's workplace is usually not oppression, but rather a condition known as endullment. Endullment is the dulling of peoples' minds as a result of their nonparticipation. It occurs in schools and it happens at work. Endullment leads to low motivation, poor attendance, refusal to cooperate to improve the system, and defeatism. Endullment conditions people to be apathetic about the world around them.

CREATING AN IMPLEMENTATION PLAN

If it is your task to help your managers become team leaders, it helps to gain their consent. This can be a slow process if they are comfortable with the status quo, even when the business may be in serious trouble. Team formation should not be something management does to people. It is a process in which people have to participate in defining and creating their own liberation. When people are not ready to accept the responsibility of becoming empowered, then there must be an educational process to set the stage for change.

When the climate is right for change, it is ideal to involve people in planning the change process. A plan is important because in spite of everyone's best efforts, there will be some leaders who want to hold on to their comfortable traditional behavior. The plan forces the organization to confront this situation. People must be challenged to either lead in a team environment, participate as an empowered team member, or find some isolated task where they do not need to work with others.

MENTORS CAN HELP

Developing a cadre of people who have already made the transition from traditional to team leadership facilitates the change process. These individuals can serve as coaches and mentors to assure that behavioral changes really take place and to guide leaders in dealing with the emotional challenges created by new leadership styles. Lockheed Martin has successfully used this concept in establishing empowered teams in its Oak Ridge facilities. Managers who showed an early ability to lead in team settings were assigned to serve as coaches and mentors for other supervisors who were making the transition to becoming team leaders.

SETTING THE BOUNDARIES

It is imperative for the team leader to clarify the work group's boundaries. Boundary definition needs to be established by management and understood by the team leader and all team members. This is a point that must be covered in any training for team leaders.

Boundaries differ from one workplace to another, but generally all groups have boundaries regarding obeying laws that apply to the workplace. Health, safety, and environmental regulations create boundaries within which teams must work. Budget restrictions often create boundaries. Different organizations have a wide range of boundaries when it comes to human resources policies. Many companies allow empowered teams to conduct their own performance appraisals, interview and hire new team members, and conduct their own discipline. Other organizations reserve those functions for the human resources organization.

It is important for the manager in a team setting to understand the need to change boundaries based on the maturity of the team and the organization's maturity in using teams. In early phases of establishing and using teams, boundaries need to be tight. Over time, as teams mature and as the organization's use of teams matures, boundaries can be expanded. It would be a mistake to launch into a team effort with wide-open boundaries for teams. It is also a mistake to keep boundaries tight after the teams have proven their ability to function and are ready to take on new tasks.

PITFALLS IN CREATING TEAM LEADERS

The major pitfall in creating team leaders occurs when organizations buy a single package or program that is supposed to transform the organization and everyone is driven through some training program like sheep through dip.

In general, organizations that have been successful in creating team environments do so by giving people autonomy and flexibility in defining the team culture that best fits their organization. Every company, every factory, every hospital, every school has a unique history and set of experiences that should be considered when launching an effort to create teams. Take full advantage of past training when designing new training for team leaders. Avoid the impression of taking off down a brand new road, and instead, focus on moving forward by weaving together the organization's existing strengths with the best of new leadership methods that are proving to be successful in other organizations.

Within Lockheed Martin, for example, site managers have a great deal of local autonomy in deciding how they will implement team activities. Sites benchmark each other and are free to benchmark other companies as well. This has led the company to receive numerous awards for manufacturing excellence and generates a strong sense of ownership of the team process within each part of the company.

If you are leading the transition process to teams, do not spend your time looking for a silver bullet or a single consultant or training program that will do it for you. Get out and benchmark other organizations, check the literature for yourself, and customize an approach that will fit your specific location.

15

Strategic Planning in a Team Environment

With teams, the process of strategic planning begins with the premise that quality and customer satisfaction are bonded together and serve as the core of the team's very being. This process fosters a vision of long-term competitive position and viability for the organization based on anticipation of customers' needs and the use of the quality discipline to effectively meet those needs.

Any effort to conduct strategic planning with teams that does not begin from the premise that the team exists to serve customers and must excel in the quality of its service will be destined to lead to failure for the team and failure for the organization using teams.

WHO TO INVOLVE IN THE PLANNING

There are two levels of strategic planning in an organization that uses a team process: strategic planning can be conducted for the overall organization, or it can occur for a specific team.

For strategic planning for an overall organization, it is vital to have representation from all the teams, or from each type of team if the organization is really large. If an organization consists of four to ten teams, then have two people from each team be involved in the strategic planning. If the organization has ten to twenty teams, then have one person represent each of the teams. If the organization has more than twenty teams (and many organizations have over a hundred teams), then select people who will represent the interests of groups of teams.

For strategic planning within a single team, it is important for all of the team members who want to participate to be part of the process.

SEVEN STEPS

In the process of strategic planning teams need to address seven broad steps. The seven steps may sound lengthy, but they can often be accomplished in a few hours. Strategic planning with teams works best when approached from a blitz-building perspective (Dew, 1997b). Get the team together and do it. Don't agonize over it and drag it out for days or weeks. You'll lose all your energy and commitment from the team if it takes too long. Overall, the process proceeds as follows:

1. The process begins with a focus on the customers' future needs.

2. The planners envision where they want to be in the future in regard to the customers' needs.

3. The vision of customer service and competitive position is then embellished with dreams of how the organization will look to the people who serve in it.

4. With this whole vision in mind, the planners scan the horizon for trends that will influence which paths best lead to the vision.

5. The gaps between the vision and the current reality are identified.

6. An implementation plan is created to achieve the vision.

7. The plan is implemented and the process is reassessed.

A key point to consider is the scope of time for the visioning exercise. Some organizations consider a plan that forecasts three years into the future to be strategic. Japanese companies often work with a vision that peers forty or more years into the future. A five-year vision is a reasonable time frame for strategic planning with a team.

WHAT WILL THE CUSTOMER WANT?

Team-based strategic planning begins with the customer in mind. The questions to ask revolve around who the customer will be, what the customer will want, and what trends will impact the customer over the coming years.

Who will the customer be? Are these customers the same ones you have today? Will they be new customers in emerging world markets? Younger? Older? More ethically diverse? Better educated? Collect data and consider how the customer base is changing.

What will the customer want? Customers want to live a better life, to be happy, to have ease and comfort and leisure time. They want to lower their costs and have reliable products and services delivered on time with no hassle. How will you meet and exceed those expectations? After all, customers did not really know that they wanted minivans, cellular phones, home computers, and faxes until someone considered how these products would improve the customers' lives.

It is critical to keep the team focused on the customer. Teams that focus inward during strategic planning are headed for disaster.

WHERE DO YOU WANT TO BE WITH THE CUSTOMERS?

Once the customers' perspective has been considered, planners should determine where the organization wants to be in relation to the customers. Does the organization want to keep the same customers, expand into new customer areas, give up, maintain, or expand market positions?

Quality should be a major factor in reaching decisions regarding positioning the organization with its customers. A successful organization will focus its energies in its areas of excellence, where high-quality service and products are provided to customers in the most profitable manner for the organization. Weak areas, such as endeavors where quality is low, scrap costs are high, or customers have complaints, must either be targeted for a quality revolution or abandoned as untenable.

WHERE DO YOU WANT TO BE AS AN ORGANIZATION?

In addition to the vision related to external factors, such as competitive position, an organization must have a vision as to what it wants to look like internally.

What are the core values of the organization that will be projected into the future? How will the organization develop and educate people? How will decisions be made? How much power will be shared with the people who do the work? How shall the company be viewed by the communities in which it works? What stand will the organization take on ethics, diversity, and compliance with laws?

The total vision for the organization's future includes the customer-related issues and the internal core values. A commitment to quality should permeate both the internal and external aspects of the organization's vision.

SCANNING THE HORIZON

When the vision is in place, it is time to scan the horizon for trends that will impact how to best achieve the vision. The organization needs a weather forecast to understand what the future conditions will be that will impact the business or service environment. Fortunately, any organization can draw upon a great deal of broad analysis of the future. Demographic studies, long term economic forecasts, and even technical projections can be used to assess the weather.

One basic weather trend to consider is a phenomenon known as "cultural radiation," a term coined by the historian Arnold Toynbee. Toynbee observed the manner in which an idea, behavior, or technology is developed in one place and then radiates to other people over time. The explosion of information means that we are experiencing global cultural radiation. If karaoke is popular in Japan, it will be in America soon, and among the Eskimos in no time.

A second weather pattern to consider is the increasing rate of change. Technology is changing more and more rapidly. Major new breakthroughs can make businesses obsolete overnight. Organizations that do not have a vision will be blown in many directions as change accelerates around them.

BUILD YOUR OWN ROAD

There is no yellow brick road waiting for any organization, just as there is no instant pudding for achieving quality. Each company must know its vision and build its own road for achieving its vision. The principal step in building the road to the future is to identify the gaps between where the organization is and where it wants to be. These gaps must be identified as specifically as possible. They may deal with the quality of a process, the satisfaction of a customer, the levels of management, the knowledge of the workers, the absence of empowerment, or other issues. The gaps will vary from one organization to the next. What is common is the necessity to close the gaps to achieve the vision.

CLOSING THE GAPS

For each gap that has been identified, there must be a plan with goals, responsibilities, and time lines. Preparation of the plan should be as participative as possible, if the organization wants support in implementing the plan. Those who have input to a plan tend to support it. This is why strategic planning in a team environment can be so effective, since it brings together the organization's stakeholders who must be committed to implementing the actions in the plan.

Closing the gaps means organizing people to take the diagnostic and remedial journeys. It often means creating new systems to support quality goals, such as peer performance review and variable compensation programs.

IMPLEMENT, TRACK, AND REASSESS

Once the plans are in place for closing the gaps, implement. This is the hard part. Implementation means devoting resources to collect data, designing changes, and overcoming the resistance to the needed changes. Implementing changes to assure high quality and customer satisfaction is akin to starting an exercise program. You know you want to exercise, you may buy the exercise equipment, clothes, and training tapes, but getting right down and doing it means hard work. The organization knows it wants high quality to assure a competitive position. There is probably no shortage of books about quality and training materials gathering dust. Today, many workers know more about improving quality than their organization will allow them to implement because it takes time.

Once implementation plans are launched, progress should be tracked. At least once a year, the planning group should meet to reassess the vision and the steps that are underway to close the gap between the vision and reality. Performance indicators regarding progress on the plan should be posted where the team can see the progress and can discuss the status of the plan during their team meetings.

FOUR BARRIERS TO STRATEGIC PLANNING IN TEAMS

Four barriers can keep organizations from starting down the path of strategic planning. These barriers, which are woven into the culture and belief system of companies that cannot take proactive steps to influence their future, include an inward focus, misunderstandings of quality, a pattern of endullment, and obsession with current problems.

AN INWARD FOCUS

If the managers of an organization are inwardly focused they will never look outside to contemplate what the customers need. Managers with inward focus believe that if things are not broken they should not be fixed. There is an unspoken belief that next year will be just like this year, and since we are okay this year, why worry about next year?

Most models of organizations depict the managers as the top of a hierarchy, but it might be more accurate to envision the manager in the center of a sphere. The outer shell of the sphere consists of people who have direct contact with customers. An inwardly focused management is content to work issues within the sphere. There is little permeability into the organization from the customers' perspectives.

QUALITY AS CONFORMANCE TO REQUIREMENTS

A broad range of perspectives and knowledge exists regarding quality, as well as many points of view about how quality should be achieved. The best strategic planning occurs in organizations that ascribe to a broad definition of quality and the integration of quality principles into every activity.

When quality is perceived to be only a reactive conformance to requirements, it ceases to be a meaningful factor in the organization's vision. Conformance to requirements is an important component of quality, but in and of itself is not a complete definition of the quality discipline. Some people are able to create proactive approaches to conformance to requirements by focusing on the customers' requirements. A broad definition of quality as a proactive philosophy and set of tools makes strategic planning possible.

A CULTURE OF ENDULLMENT

Strategic planning will not occur in a culture of endullment. Endullment is the dulling of peoples' minds as a result of their nonparticipation, which leads to low motivation, poor attendance, refusal to cooperate to improve the system, and learned apathy (Shor, 1992).

People experience endullment in the school system and at work. Once an organization has a culture of endullment it slips into a false belief in reification, the concept that a system that was created by people cannot be changed by people. People who are endulled resist the strategic planning process because they deny their own ability to influence the future. The culture of endullment treats scrap and rework as a normal part of doing work. There is no concept of continuous improvement among endulled workers and managers.

THE SISYPHUS SYNDROME

Sisyphus was the legendary figure in Greek mythology who spent all day rolling a large stone up a hill. At night the stone would roll down and he would spend the next day repeating the process.

The Sisyphus syndrome describes those organizations that are fixated on dealing with the crises de jour. If an issue is not a crisis—a stone to roll immediately up a hill—it never gets addressed. Strategic issues, by definition, never get addressed in an organization that pursues Sisyphus's focus on the crisis of the moment.

In a culture of crisis, managers have a sense of immediate accomplishment. There are action, deadlines, meetings, and excitement, which create the impression of progress. All of this activity is addictive and leads to an avoidance of both short-term and strategic planning. For Sisyphus, nothing seems to happen when people are planning. Stop this planning nonsense and get out there and put your shoulders to a boulder that we need to move today. The lack of planning creates the crises that lead to the avoidance of planning.

JUMP STARTING THE PROCESS

The quickest way to conduct a strategic planning process with a team is get the team together in a quiet setting and ask them to envision that it is five years in the future. The team is being honored as the best-performing part of the whole organization. Invite the team members to define this future state and draw out their views about how they relate to their customers and their internal processes. Then ask the team members to describe how they achieved this successful future state. This will draw out their ideas about how to develop an implementation plan to move from the current condition to the desired future state. It also helps to ask the team to identify the forces and influences that could have derailed their success in achieving the future state and weave those observations into the planning process.

ACHIEVING YOUR VISION

Strategic planning is a dynamic process that can help any organization assure competitive position through customer satisfaction by thinking in terms of quality. Effective strategic planning requires the input from stakeholders of the organization who can create a vision that encompasses the needs of the the customer and the needs of the organization. From there, the process focuses on recognizing trends that will impact the planning process, followed by the development of specific plans that will enable the vision to become reality.

As a process, strategic planning is within the grasp of any team. Although there are barriers to strategic thinking, the process itself is highly effective when employed in a team environment. With a team-centered strategic planning process, organizations are able not only to do things right, but also to do the right thing.

TEAM LEADER'S PERSPECTIVE

Regardless of the state of strategic planning in the organization, it is the team leader's job to assure that the team has a vision and strategic plan that supports the organization and drives the team to excel in meeting customer needs. The team leader must share the organization's strategic plan with the team members and carve out time for the team to develop its own strategic plan.

It is the team leader's role to keep asking the team if it is devoting its energy to the right things, from a strategic point of view. The leader must keep asking the team how it is progressing in working on the strategic issues and actions that will enable the team to make step changes in performance over time.

MIDDLE MANAGER'S PERSPECTIVE

The middle manager is in the pivot position regarding strategic planning. As Likert has pointed out, the middle manager is the linking pin that focuses the teams on achieving the organization's objectives. If the middle manager fails to share the organization's mission, vision, and strategic plan with the teams, then the teams are set up to fail (Likert, 1961)

The middle manager is responsible for insisting that each team will have a strategy for how it will support the organization's strategic plan and for making sure that teams carve out the time to do some strategic thinking. Middle managers must challenge the teams to raise the bar of performance to new heights and to accomplish step changes in performance. The middle manager achieves leverage in steering teams toward step changes by encouraging and even facilitating strategic planning sessions that will raise the energy level in teams and renew commitment to achieving the organization's objectives.

16

Managing Compliance Issues with Teams

It is no accident that the movement toward using teams in the work environment has been concurrent with an emphasis on quality in manufacturing, service organizations, and health care, and in government and educational settings. The high commitment achieved through the use of teams helps to accomplish the concept of building quality into a product advocated by Deming. Joseph Juran built his quality improvement around the concept of cross-functional teams and introduced the team concept into hundreds of organizations.

Early research into team processes conducted at the Tavistock Institute began to suggest that teams would prove to be highly effective in exercising control over quality and other compliance-related issues (Rhenman, 1968). This has proven to be the case with teams within Lockheed Martin and in many other organizations. For example, a team at a highly classified defense facility operated by Lockheed Martin assumed total responsibility for controlling thousands of top-secret documents as well as control of hazardous chemicals used in photographing and copying documents. This team won an award for taking on the process of completing eliminating their hazardous waste streams.

The Saturn plant's teams in Tennessee are responsible for their own compliance activities. Saturn teams control quality, health and safety, and waste management (Bolton, 1993). Likewise, empowered teams at Miller Brewing Company have assumed responsibility for monitoring their safety, quality, waste management, and housekeeping (Wellins et al., 1994). Teams at Hoechst Celanese have developed documentation for evaluating their safety performance (Sattizahn, 1993).

TEAMS CAN IMPROVE OSHA COMPLIANCE

Teams are a proven vehicle for improving an organization's ability to meet new and existing requirements from regulatory agencies such as OSHA. When a Navy hospital was charged with the responsibility of preparing to meet new OSHA requirements for handling materials, a self-managed team was formed to determine the best ways to meet the new requirements (Appleman and Large, 1995). The team developed methods that were considered superior by the hospital's management to previous OSHA implementations and the team continued beyond the design stage into the implementation and evaluation phase.

TEAMS AND ENVIRONMENTAL STANDARDS

Numerous examples of teams can be cited that have proven successful in helping organizations meet and exceed environmental requirements. What is new is the concept of using teams to meet new environmental programs like ISO 14000. Wheelabrator Technologies has proven the utility of forming a cross-functional team to guide that company's implementation of the 14001 standard (Hemenway and Hale, 1996). The cross-functional team approach assures that all the disciplines that must be involved in implementing an environmental management system are on board and are a party to the decision making process. The usual benefits of teams-enhanced communication, buy-in to decisions, and commitment to implement team decisions-make the team approach superior to the traditional hierarchical approach of assigning the task of achieving 14001 certification to a single manager or organization.

ERROR-FREE PERFORMANCE

Management must assure that teams have a system for controlling quality, safety, and effective environmental practices. Another way of stating this is that management and teams must work to strive for error-free performance to achieve outstanding levels of safety, quality, and conformance to environmental regulations.

It is management's role to implement a "WHAT, WHY, HOW" model (Figure 16.1) to enable teams to achieve excellence in quality and regulatory requirements. The specific requirements will obviously differ from one setting to the next, but all organizations have requirements that must be met by their teams.

It is now recognized that the use of teams can significantly enhance the control that an organization exerts over achieving regulatory requirements (Simmons, 1995). This is because team members can exercise self-control within the group, which is the essence of Deming's concept of building quality into a product or process.

WHAT, WHY, HOW

Three things that must occur to achieve high quality, error-free performance and compliance to regulatory requirements in a team setting (Figure 16.1).

Figure 16.1
What, Why, How Model

What is to be done.
Why it is important to do it this way.
How · give specific steps   · provide specific warnings about common mistakes

First, management must define what the needs are from a compliance, safety, quality, and regulatory perspective. This might include minimizing defects in products, obtaining a certain level in customer satisfaction, specific environmental requirements, and conformance to specific laws and regulations in a specific industry. These are musts for the team to achieve and are not negotiable. As a manager, you must be as specific as possible with the team. You are well advised to call on a staff specialist in health, safety, quality, and environmental protection to help define the requirements for the team.

Second, explain why the requirement is in place. What are the risks to the public, the customer, or the team members? What are the legal consequences of failure to comply? What will happen to market share and the customer base if these requirements are not met? Most people will resist a mandated requirement for themselves or the team unless they understand the rationale for the requirement. Time spent explaining why is paid back a hundredfold because it helps get buy-in people to participate.

The third step is to define how the requirements will be met. Here is where the team process again gives managers and the organization a competitive advantage over organizations that are locked into more traditional hierarchical structures. The whole team is engaged in defining how to meet and beat the requirements. This provides new ideas and strategies by harnessing the creativity of the whole team. Everyone on the team will invest time and energy in meeting the requirements.

TRACK AND TREND

The team's regulatory and quality requirements should be posted as performance indicators for tracking by the team. (Figure 16.2) The team should actively track and discuss their quality, health, safety, and environmental performance as part of their regular team meeting. The team leader needs to be on the watch for trends in the performance indicators that suggest a problem may be developing and should be ready to assist the team in conducting a root cause analysis of trends (see Chapter 11).

Figure 16.2
Team Data on Environmental Compliance

	Jan	Feb	Mar	Apr	May	Jun
Reportable Inquiries	0	0	0	1		
Off-the-job Inquiries	1	0	0	0		
MSDS Non-conformances	0	0	0	0		
Fire Extinguisher Inspections	2	2	2	2		
HAZMAT Non-compliances	0	0	0	0		
Safety Meetings	1	1	1	1		

SELF-ASSESSMENTS

It is infinitely better for an organization to discover and correct its own quality, health, safety, and environmental problems than to have a regulatory agency come in and do so. Staff specialists should work with teams to develop internal self-assessment forms that enable the team members to critique their own performance (Figure 16.3). For example, a self-assessment

Figure 16.3
Self-Assessment Form

Team: _____   Month: _____ Year: _____

	1	2	Week 3	4	5
Rejected Parts	2	1	0		
Containers of Waste	1	1	3		
"Out of Date" Tags	1	0	0		
Downtime	8hrs	2hrs	8hrs		
Attendance	100%	96%	98%		
Safety Meetings	1	1	1		
Maintenance Request	1	3	0		

form can be used by team members to verify that quality control activities are being conducted, that safety meetings are actually occurring, and to look for trends in absenteeism.

Teams should strive to achieve a "no-knock audit" status, where an outside auditor could arrive without any advance warning (no-knock) and not find any problems or deviations. Many teams in Lockheed Martin's aeronautics facilities in Orlando have achieved this ultrahigh level of quality and total compliance to regulations.

THE STAR CONCEPT

Many teams have made effective use of what is called the star concept in addressing compliance and regulatory issues. Regulatory issues are drawn as points on a star. Team members assume responsibility for each point of the star and focus on achieving excellence in that area (Figure 16.4).

Figure 16.4
Star Concept

Conduct
Safety Meetings

Inspect
Equipment

Keep
MSDS
Sheets

Test
Safety
Showers

Inspect
Fire
Extinguishers

Responsibility for a regulatory area, such as quality or safety, may rotate among the team members. In this way, each team member acquires new knowledge, and no individual is burned out by having to work on a compliance related issue year after year.

TEAM LEADER'S PERSPECTIVE

The team leader has many responsibilities related to quality, safety, health, and environmental compliance. First and foremost, the team leader must set a high standard or expectation for performance for the team. If the team leader is lax in this area, the team will likewise become lax. If the team leader sets demanding standards, the team will achieve and exceed those high standards.

Second, the team leader must help the team get the expert resources and knowledge necessary to succeed. In some cases this means bringing in the right staff person or outside resource to work with the team on solving problems or utilizing new methods to achieve a breakthrough in performance. In other cases it means finding a way to free up a team member's time to attend training that will enable him or her to serve as the team's expert on health, safety, quality, security, environmental, or other requirement.

Third, the team leader must be ready to take problems up to higher management when they are beyond the scope of what the team can handle. Some issues span beyond the team's boundaries and must be worked on by a variety of teams or by staff experts to resolve. Being quick to recognize and elevate these types of issues will help the organization remain successful in achieving regulatory excellence.

MIDDLE MANAGER'S PERSPECTIVE

Middle managers likewise have some special roles in helping their teams achieve regulatory compliance. First, middle managers must assure that the requirements are known to the teams. If the teams do not know what the rules are, they cannot be expected to meet them, and management is 100 percent responsible for defining the rules.

Second, middle managers must budget and provide the expert resources and funds for training that is needed for the teams to be fully compliant with requirements. Middle managers can see the big picture regarding requirements and can develop the most cost-effective grand strategy for providing resources.

Third, and just as important as the other two actions, middle managers must be out walking their spaces in the organization and seeing firsthand how requirements are being met. Middle managers should go out and observe how shift turnovers are being handled to assure that critical information is being passed on. They should observe whether or not performance indicators related to regulatory requirements are posted and used by the teams. They should plan on visiting work areas to briefly study logbooks and quality control records and observe safety meetings and other activities. This communicates interest and commitment in these areas that reinforces team behaviors. The middle manager should complement teams for excellent performance observed during walk-throughs and should coach team leaders when team performance is not meeting expectations.

17

Creativity and Teams

A great deal of research in the field of cognitive psychology has emerged over the last decade to suggest that an individual's performance can be influenced by moods and emotions (Goleman, 1995). In the team environment we find that individuals' "ups and downs" influence team performance as well. There is good reason to consider the role of stress and creativity in the performance of teams and the manager's role in stimulating creative thought.

ANXIETY AND HYPOMANIA

Anxiety, brought on by stress, will undermine job performance and academic performance of all kinds. When team members feel overwhelmed and overburdened they will turn on each other in outbursts of anger. A negative atmosphere will quickly grow within the team and a self- fulfilling prophecy of defeat and resignation will quickly emerge. On the other hand, hypomania (a mild state of euphoria) can induce a climate of optimal performance for individuals in the team that generates high energy among team members, resulting in a synergy that impels the team to new levels of performance.

It behooves the team leader and the team members, then, to strive for achieving a condition that in the language of cognitive psychology is known as a state of flow, or peak performance (Goleman, 1995). See Table 17.1.

Table 17.1
Attributes of Flow (Peak Performance)

- Positive emotions
- High energy levels
- Emotions aligned with tasks

In a state of flow, individuals are emotionally positive about the work they are performing. Their energy level is high, and this high energy and positive emotional state is focused on getting their work done. While there is little scientific information on the effect of flow within a team, field observations suggest that flow can be contagious. One team member who is "up" can bring other team members up to a state of flow. This phenomenon has been widely observed in team activities in sports and appears to hold true in the work arena as well.

THE MANAGER'S ROLE IN STIMULATING FLOW

The manager's role is to create an environment that maximizes flow and to encourage employees to achieve hypomania. The manager can take several specific actions to encourage and stimulate flow (Table 17.2).

Table 17.2
Management Actions to Stimulate Flow

Encourage	Praise the group
Stimulate	Point out opportunities/needs for creative thinking and ideas
Push	Raise the bar on performance expectations and encourage people to get out of the box
Educate	Offer creative thinking tools

Management should encourage groups to think creatively by giving them praise and recognition for new solutions to problems and for getting out of the current thinking box. Coming up with new, creative ideas means taking some risk, such as the risk of being ridiculed for a new idea, or the risk of having an idea fail. The manager can help reduce this risk by giving praise to groups that have been willing to take the risk for coming up with new ideas.

Managers should stimulate creative thinking by pointing out places or situations where new ideas are needed. Old problems, new situations, and any form of change provide the opportunity for coming up with new ideas for being more effective, making better use of resources, and finding new ways to get things done. Managers can be very specific by pointing out problems or issues and inviting a team to come up with some out of the box ideas for dealing with the issue.

Managers often need to push teams into being more creative. It is the leader's role to raise the bar on individual and team performance, and this includes pushing a team to get out of the box and come up with new ideas. Often it takes only a slight nudge to get a team to overcome their inertia, but sometimes the leader must be willing to get in the team members' faces and confront them with the need to make a breakthrough. This is leadership. The leader must always be vigilant about not slipping into a laissez-faire mode and allowing teams to get by with mundane performance when they are capable of developing new and exciting ways of performing work.

Finally, the manager may need to educate the team members in a variety of tools that can stimulate creative thinking. Most people have heard of brainstorming, but it often does not work very well. Some additional tools might be needed to get the creative juices flowing and to stimulate some out-of-the-box thinking.

PERFORMANCE MAPS

Performance maps are a tool that can assist teams in a variety of ways. Development of a performance map can enable a team to:

1. Assess its strengths and weaknesses;

2. Identify areas for strategic focus;

3. Identify resources that can be reallocated or refocused;

4. Think about the customer's perspective and needs; and

5. Serve as a consensus process that stimulates self-assessment and strategic planning.

Steps in developing a performance map include:

1. List the functions your team performs.

2. On a scale of 10 to 1 (10 is high, 1 is low) rate how well your team performs all the functions.

3. On a scale of 10 to 1 (10 is high, 1 is low) rate the importance of each function your team performs.

4. Form a graph that shows the relationship of importance to performance, where the vertical axis shows performance and the horizontal axis shows importance.

5. Map your data on importance and performance onto the graph.

6. Develop team strategies based on the performance map.

The process begins by involving the team in identifying the work they are currently performing. Through discussion the team members then rate how well they are currently performing these functions. (Note that this is a rating process, not a ranking process. For example, in ranking from 10 down to 1, you would go 10, 9, 8, 7, 6, 5, 4, 3, 2, 1. In rating, you may have more than one factor that you would rate as a 9, while you may not have any you would rate as a 7.)

After the team has rated its performance, consider the relative importance of the work the team performs. Rate each item according to its performance and give it a numerical value on the scale of 10 down to 1. After both performance and importance have been rated by the team, the data can be placed on a graph (Figure 17.1) that compares performance on the vertical axis to importance on the horizontal axis.

Strategies can be developed based on what the data shows. Work that is

Figure 17.1
Graph of Performance and Importance

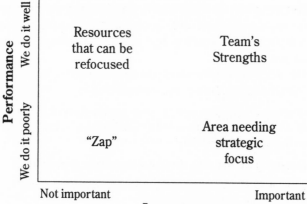

done well and is important is the team's current value-adding strength. This work needs to be maintained and resources to do this work should be protected. The team might also be able to share knowledge in this area with other groups, and might look for ways to expand their work in this quadrant.

Work that is important, but not done well, comprises the area for strategic focus within the team. The team needs to explore why it is not performing well, develop a plan for improvement, implement the improvement plan, and then evaluate the progress of the implementation plan. Over time, work functions in this quadrant need to move up into the quadrant of value-adding strengths.

Work that is done well but is not important makes up the resources that can be refocused. The team might look at reducing time and attention paid to work in this area. Resources used on tasks in this quadrant might be moved to work on issues in the strategic focus zone.

Work that is not done well and is not important sits in the "zap" zone. This work should be eliminated by the team. The team needs to stop wasting time and energy on activities in this area.

MOUNTAIN CLIMBING

Mountain climbing is another creative thinking tool that the manager or team leader can introduce to teams to stimulate creative ideas (Figure 17.2). The purpose of mountain climbing is to focus the team on issues, establish team ownership of issues, build a common language about a situation, and stimulate new and creative ways to solve a problem or deal with a situation.

Mountain climbing can be applied to a variety of team situations. Teams might use it to find a new way to perform a task, or to develop new ideas for customers. Problem solving is often an issue of coming up with a new perspective in which to frame an issue, and can be like seeing a new way to cross a mountain. The mountain climbing tool is based on the old Chinese proverb that there are many mountains up to heaven and many pathways up each mountain. The team is encouraged to find as many pathways up and over the mountain as possible.

For team mountain climbing, use an easel pad and markers or make use of a chalk board or slick board, following these steps:

1. Draw a picture of where you are now with an issue and the desired future state or condition. This can also be expressed as moving from Point A (here and now) to Point B (the desired future).

2. Draw the mountain that is between the current state and the future state.

3. Think of low-altitude and high-altitude paths across the mountain and list them where everyone can see them.

   a. Low-Altitude Ideas: Low in risk Pretty normal approaches

   b. High-Altitude Ideas: Wild and crazy ideas

4. Have fun while doing this.

5. Select the best pathway across the mountain.

Figure 17.2
Mountain Climbing Metaphor

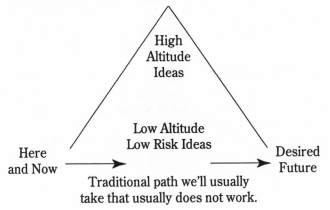

Sometimes the high-altitude ideas are real winners that the team can use. Often, the high-altitude ideas may not be practical, but they stimulate the recognition of low-altitude ideas from the team. It behooves the team to develop as many ideas as possible before honing in on selecting the best idea.

MIND MAPS

Mind maps are effective tools for helping teams organize ideas and concepts (Figure 17.3). Mind maps stimulate creative thinking and dialogue about team issues. Their purpose in the team setting is to help the team organize their thoughts, visually arrange information where it can be discussed, stimulate creative thinking, and stimulate discussion.

The following steps are used to develop a mind map, which should be drawn on an easel pad or slick board.

1. Develop a central theme and display it in the center of the map, using an image or picture to symbolize the theme.

2. Identify the major categories or themes and include them on the map, using a drawing or image for each one.

3. Use solid lines to connect the themes to the central concept.

4. Always print any writing on the mind map.

5. Use lots of colors in preparing the mind map.

6. Expand the details under each major heading by getting ideas from the team.

Figure 17.3
Mind Map of Customer Satisfaction

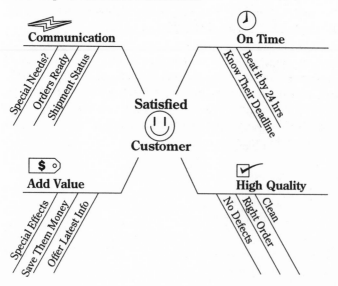

The mind map is a powerful tool for stimulating creative thinking because it draws on both the left-brain and right-brain thinking processes (Buzan, 1989). The left side of the brain is stimulated by the orderly layout of ideas through the use of print and lines. The right side of the brain is stimulated by the use of colors and pictures.

KINESTHETIC EXERCISES

Brainstorming exercises often fall flat within a team when the dynamics are poor for creative thinking. This occurs when people are not having fun, when they've been sitting down for a while (their blood is not flowing), and when their energy level is low. Because many people think and learn best when they are moving and able to draw fully on their senses, exercise and movement helps brainstorming by providing the team with kinesthetic props that will generate some fun and give people a tactile stimulus to fire up their synapses.

Examples of good kinesthetic props to stimulate brainstorming in teams are yo-yos, Play-Dough, building blocks, and any type of small, squeezable ball that people can hold in their hands and toss at one another without hurting anyone. Make these toys available and stand back as people grab an object that gives them pleasure by connecting them with lots of past positive memories and experiences. Play-Dough, for example, has a distinct smell that can take an adult back to childhood memories at age four. Allow the team members to work with their "toys" for a few minutes, and then focus them in doing a brainstorming exercise.

Experts in creative thinking have noted that having fun is fundamental to the creative process (Hall, 1995). Providing team members with kinesthetic aids is both fun and a sound method based on established patterns and preferences that people have for processing information.

It pays for the team leader and manager to encourage and push teams into being creative. In fact, teams look to management for permission to get out of the box in developing new innovations that can save money, better satisfy customers, and open up new market opportunities. The manager either will be unaware of his or her role in stimulating creative thought (and probably send signals that discourage creativity) or will be an active agent in encouraging teams to be creative.

18

Evaluating Team Effectiveness

Since a great deal of time and money can be invested in organizing and training teams, mangers will want to know whether or not the teams are functioning effectively as an organizational resource. This chapter explores some of reasons why teams fail and offers methods for evaluating teams to enhance their performance and contribution to the organization.

WHY TEAMS FAIL

Teams fail for many reasons. Sometimes teams fail due to problems with the purpose of the team if goals are unclear, and objectives keep changing. Other teams fail because they are not supported by management and their role and accountability is not well defined. In some cases, there is ineffective leadership within the team. And in other cases, there is no team centered method for rewarding performance (McGivern and Bryant, 1998).

In cases where team goals are unclear, it is necessary to revisit the issue of developing a mission statement for the team that is linked to the organization's overall mission, as stated in Chapter One. It is also essential to reexamine the team's use of performance indicators to ensure that the team has an effective method for examining its performance, as covered in Chapter Two.

When objectives keep changing in an organization communications with the teams becomes extremely important. If change is driven by market forces and customer needs, then this must be communicated quickly and effectively to the teams. If the change is driven due to a change in leadership, then the new leadership needs to make contact with the teams and share the new areas of emphasis so that the teams can adjust their activities.

In cases where teams do not seem to be working effectively with one another, managers need to examine several issues. First, how are the teams being rewarded? Is there some obvious or subtle manner in which the teams are being encouraged or rewarded for not cooperating? Is so, change it. What are the lines of communication between the teams? Is it difficult for the team members to communicate effectively in order to understand what each team needs for a win? Is there a need for a teambuilding intervention between the members of the conflicting teams? Re-examine the issues raised in Chapter Four on the interdependence.

Sometimes an organization will establish a team structure without all of the managers being on board and supportive of the team concept. In this case the organization can benefit from training that will enable managers to understand the multiple advantages of team processes (Dew, 1997a). It will be beneficial to re-examine the thoughts on creating team leaders in Chapter Fourteen as well.

In some cases teams fail due to poor execution of the nuts and bolts of team activities. Ineffective decision making practices, poorly organized meetings that waste time, conflict between team members, and the inability to use basic problem solving tools can all undermine the effectiveness of a team. These are all problems that can be avoided by investing in basic team training and are all addressed in various chapters. If these problems become apparent in an organization, the manager should re-visit the initial team training and make sure it was complete. Remedial training for a team can be useful to correct specific performance problems.

Ineffective leadership can also undermine the team effort. Managers that do not walk the talk can voice support for teams while taking actions that negate the team process. This is a tricky situation. If you, as a manager, want your teams to work, but are subverting your teams through your actions, how do you recognize this and deal with it? Team members may be reluctant to tell you. The best approach is to bring in a third party, perhaps from another team or from a staff group. Ask this person to meet with the team and assess their performance and find out what the barriers to effective team work may be. Tell the third party not to hesitate to tell you if you are the barrier. Ask for feedback and help that will enable you to become the most effective leader you can be in a team environment.

Teams fail when they are an ancillary part of the organizational structure and thought process. When teams are not a core part of the organization's strategic planning process and everyday work planning, then the teams can be held in low esteem by managers and given low priority in all aspects of planning, organization, and control of work. If this is the case, re-examine the concepts in Chapter Fifteen on strategic planning in a team environment.

Sometimes teams will fail due to problems with the support systems, such as compensation. In these cases, managers should work to redesign the support system through an action research process (Dew, 1997a).

Employ representatives from the teams to work as a team to redesign the support systems so that they serve as enablers and reinforcers instead of barriers to team-oriented behaviors.

EVALUATING TEAMS

There are two ways to evaluate teams. One approach is to examine the health of a team by assessing its activities and structure. The second approach is to examine its results. This is similar in thought to the evaluating the maintenance function of the team and the task function of the team as identified in Chapter Nine.

To evaluate the health of a team, consider the concept of phase movement of teams introduced in Chapter Nine. Phase movement is the theory that teams transition through a variety of predictable phases over the life of a team. There are at least a dozen approaches to identifying and classifying the phase movement of teams (Knowles and Knowles, 1972).

For this book, a five phase method has been identified which finds teams moving through a start-up phase, a testing phase, a performance phase, a re-testing phase, and a close-out phase, all described in Chapter Nine.

Managers can use health charts to evaluate the well-being of their teams in each one of these phases (Table 18.1). In the start-up phase the manager can check off whether or not the team has a mission statement, clear leaders, boundaries, training, a meeting place, and representation of all the stakeholders. The manager can also check to make sure that a formational meeting has occurred and that the team has conducted an initial assessment of their situation.

Table 18.1
Health Chart for Start-Up Phase

Mission statement	Yes	No
All stakeholders included	Yes	No
Boundaries defined	Yes	No
Training conducted	Yes	No
Formational meeting	Yes	No
Meeting room available	Yes	No
Situation appraisal	Yes	No

In the testing phase, the manager can evaluate whether or not a team is meeting regularly and if the attendance at the meetings is adequate (Table 18.2). Is the team using consensus decision making? What is the state of the team members emotional bank accounts? The manager can assess the presence of dysfunctional team behaviors, such as diverting, blocking, attacking, dominating, and withdrawing, as explained in Chapter Nine. Is the team using performance indicators? And is the team achieving some win-win accomplishments that are benefiting the organization?

Table 18.2
Health Chart for Teams in Testing Phase

Regular meetings	Yes	No	
Consensus decision making	Yes	No	
Performance indicators used	Yes	No	
Early accomplishments	Yes	No	
Attendance	High	Medium	Low
Emotional bank accounts	High	Medium	Low
Dysfunctional behaviors	High	Medium	Low

When teams mature into the performance phase, managers should check on a number of team behaviors and attributes in order to keep the team healthy (Table 18.3). Does the team continue to meet regularly? Are the meetings well attended? Is the team's sphere of influence narrow or broad? Has the team's success been recognized? Are the team's activities being reviewed by management? Are dysfunctional behaviors emerging? Could the team benefit from additional training in areas such as creativity or from on-going teambuilding activities?

Table 18.3
Health Chart for Teams in the Performance Phase

Regular meetings	Yes	No	
Progress reviewed by management	Yes	No	
Success recognized	Yes	No	
Continued teambuilding needed?	Yes	No	
Creativity training needed?	Yes	No	
Attendance	High	Medium	Low
Dysfunctional behaviors	High	Medium	Low
Sphere of team's influence	Broad	Narrow	

Finally, managers need to assess whether a team has moved into a re-testing phase and needs to be re-charged, or whether a team is in a close-out phase and needs to be brought to closure (Table 18.4). It is important for managers to determine if the team can be re-invigorated by bringing in new leadership. Does the team need to conduct a new appraisal of their situation in order to find new issues to work? What is the status of the emotional bank account of the team members? Has the team fallen into a pattern of dysfunctional behavior? Is there a need to formally close the team?

Table 18.4
Health Chart for the Re-testing and Close-out Phases

New leadership needed?	Yes	No
New situation appraisal needed?	Yes	No

Emotional bank accounts	High	Medium	Low
Dysfunctional behaviors	High	Medium	Low
Closure needed?	Yes	No	

Understanding the health of teams can be an important data point in evaluating the effectiveness of teams. An unhealthy team will rarely function at its most effective possible level of performance and output for the organization. However, just because a team is healthy, there is no absolute assurance that it is fully effective. Managers should always keep an eye on the bottom line indicators of success, such as costs, quality, volume of output, and meeting schedule.

USE OF SURVEYS TO DETERMINE THE HEALTH OF TEAMS

Another approach to determining the effectiveness of teams is to use a standardized survey. There are a variety of team surveys on the market that can be used. University Associates, in San Diego, California, offers a variety of instruments that can be used.

Surveys can give very useful feedback to managers regarding the health and effectiveness of teams in a stable work environment. If there is a great deal of change, the survey needs to be administered in a way that will allow outside changes to be factored out of the survey results. This is done by administering the survey twice, in a before and after manner, and to give the survey to a control group as well as a target group.

For example, if a manager is introducing teams to an organization and wants data on the benefits of creating teams, then a survey can be used that is given to the people in the work group prior to formation of the team and after the team has been formed. This provides a before and after view of the results of forming a team. At the same time, the same survey can be given to a work group that is not becoming a team. This serves as a control group and they also take the survey twice. Changes in the organization, such as the introduction of a new accounting system, can then be factored out of the results of the survey for the team, since the results will also be seen in the non-team work group.

EXAMPLE OF TEAM HEALTH SURVEY

The Appendix to this chapter offers an example of a team health survey form. The survey is designed so that it can be completed by a team leader, a team member, or the customer of the team. This gives a variety of perspectives regarding the health of the teams. The survey is designed to focus on issues that are proven to cause teams to fail.

APPENDIX
Team Health Survey

TEAM : _____ DATE:_____

Survey being completed by a: 1. Team Member
                                 2. Team Leader
                                 3. Team Customer

For each item, circle the numerical response
that best describes your view of the team.

	Strongly Disagree				Strongly Agree
1. The mission of this team is clearly defined.	1	2	3	4	5
2. The team uses performance indicators or other data to measure its performance.	1	2	3	4	5
3. The team involves all the important stakeholders that need to be represented.	1	2	3	4	5
4. The team has regular meetings.	1	2	3	4	5
5. The team is providing results that benefit the plant and the team's customers.	1	2	3	4	5
6. Management knows what the team is working on.	1	2	3	4	5
7. The team is working on issues that are important to the plant.	1	2	3	4	5
8. The team makes decisions through consensus.	1	2	3	4	5
9. Team meetings are well attended.	1	2	3	4	5
10. The team is recognized by management for the work it is doing.	1	2	3	4	5
11. Overall, the plant supports the use of teams.	1	2	3	4	5

12. Team members work well together.   1 2 3 4 5

13. The team is solving difficult problems.   1 2 3 4 5

14. Having the team has improved communication with   1 2 3 4 5
    customers and support groups.

15. The team can get the necessary resources that   1 2 3 4 5
    are needed to implement their ideas.

How can this team be more effective?

_____

_____

_____

_____

Bibliography

Adams, Frank and Hansen, Gary. 1987. *Putting Democracy to Work*. Eugene, Ore.: Hulogos' Communications.

Altizer, Christopher C. 1993. "Four Steps to Empowerment." *Tapping the Network Journal* (Spring): 21–23.

American Productivity Center. 1986. *Designing Effective Work Teams*. Houston, Tex.: American Productivity Center.

Appleman, Kaye, and Large, Kris. 1995. "Navy Hospital Fights Disease with a Quality Team." *Quality Progress* (April): 47–49.

Aubrey, Charles, and Felkins, Patricia. 1988. *Teamwork: Involving People in Quality and Productivity Improvement*. Milwaukee, Wis.: Quality Press.

Avery, Michel, et al. 1981. *Building United Judgment*. Madison, Wis.: Center for Conflict Resolution.

Bader, Gloria E., and Bloom, Audrey E. and Chang, Richard Y. 1996. *Measuring Team Performance*. Irvine, Calif.: Richard Chang Associates.

Bate, Paul, and Mangham, Ian. 1981. *Exploring Participation*. New York: John Wiley and Sons.

Bean, Audrey. 1986. "Including the Supervisor in Employee Involvement Efforts." *National Productivity Review* (Winter): 64–77.

Bean, William C. 1993. *Strategic Planning That Makes Things Happen*. Amherst, Mass.: Human Resource Development Press.

Beck, Gustav. 1935. "The Men of Antigonish." *Journal of Adult Education* 7: 2.

Bee, Helen L. 1987. *The Journey of Adulthood*. New York: Macmillan.

Belei, Judy, et al. 1991. "Starting Problem Solving Teams," in *Assembling and Updating Your TQM Toolkit*. Schaumburg, Ill.: Quality and Productivity Management Association.

Bemowski, Karen. 1996. "VIA Rail Puts the Breaks on Runaway Operations." *Quality Progress* (October): 37–42.

Benne, Kenneth D, and Sheats, Paul. 1948. "Functional Roles of Group Members." *Journal of Social Issues* (Spring): 51–59.

Bixler, Bob. 1993. "Empowered Measurement Systems: Catalyst for Improvement." *Tapping the Network Journal* (Summer): 17–21.

Bloomquist, Al, and McClary, Nancy. 1993. "From Supervision to Coaching," in *Empowerment: Unleashing the Full Potential of Your TQM Effort.* Schaumburg, Ill.: Quality and Productivity Management Association.

Bolton, Jane. 1993. "Establishing Boundaries for Employee Empowerment," in *Empowerment: Unleashing the Full Potential of Your TQM Effort.* Schaumburg, Ill.: Quality and Productivity Management Association.

Bolz, Bev, and Masterson, Michael. 1990. "Teams and Their Support Systems," in *Third Annual Hunter Conference on Quality Proceedings.* Madison, Wis.: Madison Area Quality Improvement Network.

Bowman, Joseph C. 1990. "Developing and Sustaining Employee Involvement," in *Third Annual Hunter Conference on Quality Proceedings.* Madison, Wis.: Madison Area Quality Improvement Network.

Bradford, Leland P, and Lippitt, Ronald. 1945. "Building a Democratic Work Group." *Personnel* 22: 3.

Buzan, Tony. 1989. *Use Both Sides of Your Brain.* New York: Penguin Books..

Byham, W. C., and Cox, Jeff. 1988. *Zapp!: The Lightning of Empowerment.* New York: Harmony.

Cartwright, Dorwin P., and Lippett, Ronald. 1957. "Group Dynamics and the Individual." *Group Psychotherapy* (January): 11–14.

Chang, Richard Y. 1994. *Building A Dynamic Team.* Irvine, Calif.: Richard Chang Associates.

Chang, Richard Y. 1994. *Success Through Teamwork.* Irvine, Calif.: Richard Chang Associates.

Clark, Jennifer. 1993. "Empowerment Within." *Tapping the Network Journal* (Spring): 14–17.

Coady, Moses. 1939. *Masters of Their Own Destiny.* New York: Harper and Brothers.

Council for Continuous Improvement. 1992. *Team Member's Handbook.* New York: Quality Resources Press.

Covey, Stephen R. 1989. *The 7 Habits of Highly Effective People.* New York: Simon & Schuster.

Davis, Philip A. 1981. "Building a Workable Participative Management System." *Management Review* (March): 26–39.

Davis, Robert A. 1993. "Delight Makes the Difference," in *Empowerment: Unleashing the Full Potential of Your TQM Effort.* Schaumburg, Ill.: Quality and Productivity Management Association.

Deming, W. Edwards. 1986. *Out of the Crisis.* Cambridge: Massachusetts Institute of Technology.

Denison, Daniel. 1982. "Sociotechnical Design and Self-Managing Work Groups." *Journal of Occupational Behavior* (October): 297–314.

Dew, John R. 1997a. *Empowerment and Democracy in the Workplace.* Westport, Conn.: Quorum Books.

Dew, John R. 1997b. *Quality Centered Strategic Planning.* New York: Quality Resources Press.

Dewey, John. 1916. *Democracy and Education.* New York: Macmillan Free Press.

Dumaine, Brian. 1990. "Who Needs A Boss?" *Quality Digest* (June): 53–64.

Dutton, Barbara. 1989. "Employee Involvement: How It Works." *Quality Digest* (June): 46–55.

Dyer, William G. 1987. *Team Building.* Reading Mass.: Addison Wesley.

Emery, Fred, and Thorsrud, Einar. 1976. *Democracy at Work.* Leiden: Martinus Nijhoff.

Faris, Nadir. 1993. "Employees Design Site Recognition System." *Tapping the Network Journal* (Spring): 18–22.

Fisher, Roger, and Ury, William. 1981. *Getting to Yes.* New York: Penguin Books.

Fitzsimmons, Charles F. 1996. "The Bossless Performance Review." *Quality Progress* (June): 77–81.

Fleming, Michael. 1994. "Entergy Turns the Corner in Total Quality Implementation with Natural Work Teams." *Tapping the Network Journal.* (Summer): 13–18.

Freire, Paulo. 1985. *The Politics of Education.* South Hadley, Mass.: Bergin and Garvey.

French, Debra G., and Hermansen, Katherine L. 1997. "Reducing Turnaround Time At SwedishAmerican Hospital," in *The Power of Empowerment.* Arlington Heights, Il.: Pride Publications.

Furtado, Thomas. 1988. "Training for a Different Management Style" *Personnel Management* (March): 40–43.

Galagan, Patricia. 1986. "Work Teams That Work." *Training and Development Journal* (November): 33–35.

Gantt, Henry. 1916. *Industrial Leadership.* New Haven: Yale University Press.

Gastil, John. 1993. *Democracy in Small Groups.* Philadelphia: New Society Publishers.

Gilbert, Gaye E. 1991. "Be Bold and Be Right," in *CASE.* Houston, Tex.: American Productivity and Quality Center.

Goldratt, Eliyahu M., and Cox, Jeff. 1984. *The Goal.* Great Barrington, Mass.: North River Press.

Goleman, Daniel. 1995. *Emotional Intelligence.* New York: Bantam Books.

Gonnodo, Bill, ed. 1997. *The Power of Empowerment.* Arlington Heights, Ill.: Pride Publications.

Griffin, Donna S. 1993. "Making a Measurable Difference Through Empowerment." *Tapping the Network Journal* (Summer): 2–4.

Guzzo, Richard A., and Salas, Eduardo. 1995. *Team Effectiveness and Decision Making in Organizations.* San Francisco, Jossey-Bass.

Hall, Doug. 1995. *Jump Start Your Brain.* New York: Warner Books.

Hammerstone, James, and Barley, Gilbert. 1990. "Lessons Learned in Setting Up Work Teams." *Tapping the Network Journal* (Spring): 7–11.

Hemenway, Caroline G., and Hale, Gregory J. 1996. "The TQEM-ISO 14001 Connection." *Quality Progress* (June): 29–32.

Herrmann, Ned. 1996. *The Whole Brain Business Book.* New York: McGraw-Hill.

Hicks, Robert F., and Bone, Diane. 1990. *Self-Managing Teams.* Los Altos, Calif.: Crisp Publishing.

Howell, Johnna L. 1995. *Tools for Facilitating Team Meetings.* Seattle: Integrity Publishing.

Hunter, Dale, Bailey, Anne and Taylor, Bill. 1992. *The Art of Facilitation.* Tucson, Ariz.: Fisher Books.

Hunter, Dale, Bailey, Anne and Taylor, Bill. 1995. *The Zen of Groups.* Tucson, Ariz.: Fisher Books.

Jackson, Tom. 1982. "Forging the Workteam: Beyond Quality Circles." *National Productivity Review* (Spring): 192–203.

Janis, Irving. 1972. *Victims of Group Think.* Boston: Houghton Mifflin Co.

Jenkins, David H. 1948. "Feedback and Group Self-Evaluation." *Journal of Social Issues* (Spring): 81–90.

Jerome, Paul J. 1994. *Re-Creating Teams During Transitions.* Irvine, Calif.: Richard Chang Associates.

Jung, Carl G. 1923. *Psychological Types.* New York: Pantheon Books.

Juran, Joseph. 1964. *Managerial Breakthrough.* New York: McGraw-Hill.

Kaner, Sam. 1996. *Facilitator's Guide to Participatory Decision Making.* Gabriolin Island, British Columbia: New Society Press.

Katkaveck, Frank, and Mallamo, Reginald. 1993. "Why, What, and How Its Going," in *Empowerment: Unleashing the Full Potential of Your TQM Effort.* Schaumburg, Ill.: Quality and Productivity Management Association.

Katzenbach, Jon R., and Smith, Douglas K. 1994. *The Wisdom of Teams.* New York: HarperCollins Books.

Kaye, Harvey. Decision Power. 1992. Englewood Cliffs, N.J.: Prentice-Hall.

Kelly, P. Keith. 1994. *Team Decision-Making Techniques.* Irvine, Calif.: Richard Chang Associates.

Kepner, Benjamin, and Tregoe, Charles. 1981. *The New Rational Manager.* Princeton, N.J.: Princeton Research Press.

Keppler, Robert. 1078. "What the Supervisor Should Know about Participative Management." *Supervisory Management* (May): 34–40.

Klein, Gerald. 1986. "Employee Centered Productivity and QWL Programs." *National Productivity Review* (Autumn): 348–362.

Klein, Janice. 1984. "Why Supervisors Resist Employee Involvement." *Harvard Business Review* (September): 87–95.

Knowles, Malcolm, and Knowles, Hulda. 1972. *Introduction to Group Dynamics.* New York: Follett Publishing.

Landes, Les. 1995. "Leading the Duck at Mission Control." *Quality Progress* (July): 43–48.

Lauck, W. Jett. 1926. *Political and Industrial Democracy: 1776–1926.* New York: Funk and Wagnalls.

Lawler, Edward. 1988a. *High Involvement Management.* San Francisco: Jossey-Bass.

Lawler, Edward. 1988b. "Substitutes for Hiearchy." *Organizational Dynamics* (Summer): 5–15.

Leana, Carrie. 1987. "Power Relinquishment Versus Power Sharing: Theoretical Clarification and Empirical Comparison of Delegation and Participation." *Journal of Applied Psychology:* 228–233.

Lee, Chris. 1990. "Beyond Teamwork." *Quality Digest* (August): 20–39.

Leo, Richard. 1996. "Xerox 2000: From Survival to Opportunity." *Quality Progress* (March): 65–71.

Lewin, Kurt. 1945. "The Practicality of Democracy." *Human Nature and Enduring Peace.* Boston: Houghton Mifflin.

Likert, Rensis. 1961. *New Patterns of Management.* New York: McGraw-Hill.

Lindeman, Eduard. 1926. *The Meaning of Adult Education.* New York: New Republic Books.

Locke, Edwin, et al. 1986. "Participation in Decision Making: When Should It Be Used?" *Organizational Dynamics* (Winter): 65–79.

Lovrich, Nicholas. 1985. "The Dangers of Participative Management." *Review of Public Personnel Administration* (Summer): 9–25.

McGivern, Michael, and Bryant, J.D. 1998. *Keeping Your Teams Afloat in the Sea of Change.* Bridgeville, Penn.: Development Design International.

Mandl, Vladimir. 1990. "Teaming Up for Performance." *Quality Digest* (September): 42–53.

Marchington, Mick. 1980. *Responses to Participation at Work.* Westmead, England: Gower Press.

Marrow, Alfred. 1976. *Management by Participation.* New York: Harper and Row.

Marsick, Victoria J. 1990. "Action Learning and Reflection in the Workplace," in *Fostering Critical Reflection in Adulthood,* ed. Jack Mezirow. San Francisco: Jossey-Bass.

Mayo, Elton. 1945. *The Social Problems of Industrial Civilization.* Andover, Mass.: Andover Press.

Meyer, Christopher. 1994. "How the Right Measures Help Teams Excel." *Harvard Business Review* (May-June): 95–103.

Mezirow, Jack. 1990. *Fostering Critical Reflection in Adulthood.* San Francisco: Jossey-Bass.

Miller, Lawrence. 1985. "Creating the New High-Commitment Culture." *Supervisory Management* (August): 21–28.

Milliken, Weston. 1996. "The Eastman Way." *Quality Progress* (October): 57–62.

Mink, Oscar G., Mink, Barbara P., and Owen, Keith Q. 1987. *Groups at Work.* Englewood Cliffs, N.J.: Educational Technology Publications.

Mitroff, Ian, and Linstone, Harold. 1993. *The Unbounded Mind.* New York: Oxford University Press.

Mohrman, Susan. 1993. "Empowerment: There's More to It Than Meets the Eye." *Tapping the Network Journal* (Spring): 14–17.

Mohrman, Susan Albers, Cohen, Susan G., and Mohrman, Allan M. 1995. *Designing Team-Based Organizations.* San Francisco: Jossey-Bass.

Mosley, Donald C. 1974. "Nominal Grouping as an Organizational Development Intervention Technique." *Training and Development Journal* (March): 30–37.

Murphy, John J. 1993. *Pulling Together: The Power of Teamwork.* Grand Rapids, Mich.: Venture Management Consultants.

Myers, Selma G. 1996. *Team Building For Diverse Work Groups.* Irvine, Calif.: Richard Chang Associates.

Nadkarni, R. A. 1995. "A Not-So-Secret Recipe for Successful TQM." *Quality Progress* (November): 91–96.

O'Reilly, Michelle, and Lesley, Bonnie. 1993. "Empowerment Practices in Educational Environments," in *Empowerment: Unleashing the Full Potential of Your TQM Effort.* Schaumburg, Ill.: Quality and Productivity Management Association.

Palmero, Richard C., and Watson, Gregory H., eds. 1993. *A World of Quality: Business Transformation at Xerox.* Rochester, N.Y.: Xerox Corp.

Parker, Glenn M. 1994. *Cross-Functional Teams.* San Francisco: Jossey-Bass.

Parker, Glenn M. 1990. *Team Players and Teamwork.* San Francisco: Jossey-Bass.

Parry, Scott B. 1994. *From Managing to Empowering.* New York: Quality Resources Press.

Pasmore, William. 1988. *Designing Effective Organizations.* New York: John Wiley and Sons.

Pierce, Richard. 1986. *Involvement Engineering.* Milwaukee: ASQC Press.

Rau, Herbert. 1995. "15 Years and Still Going." *Quality Progress* (July), 57–59.

Rees, Fran. 1991. *How to Lead Work Teams.* San Diego: Pfeiffer & Co..

Rhenman, Eric. 1968. *Industrial Democracy and Industrial Management.* London: Tavistock Press.

Richardson, Peter. 1985. "Courting Greater Employee Involvement through Participative Management." *Sloan Management Review* (Winter): 33–44.

Rogers, Carl. 1961. *On Becoming a Person.* Boston: Houghton Mifflin.

Rothstein, Lawrence. 1995. "The Empowerment Effort That Came Undone." *Harvard Business Review* (January-February): 20–31.

Rubinstein, Sidney. 1987. *Participative Systems at Work.* New York: Human Sciences Press.

Russell, Peter. 1979. *The Brain Book.* New York: Penguin Books.

Ryan, Bobbie. 1995. "Naval Station Mayport Jump-starts Quality." *Quality Progress* (July): 95–100.

Sattizahn, John. 1993. "Measuring SDT Service Effectiveness," in *Empowerment: Unleashing the Full Potential of Your TQM Effort.* Schaumburg, Ill.: Quality and Productivity Management Association.

Scholtes, Peter R. 1988. *The Team Handbook.* Madison, Wis.: Joiner Associates.

Scott, Cynthia, and Jaffe, Dennis. 1991. *Empowerment.* Los Altos, Calif.: Crisp Publications.

Selekman, Ben. 1924. *Employe's Representation in Steel Works.* New York: Russell Sage Foundation.

Shonk, James. 1992. *Team-Based Organizations: Developing a Successful Team Environment.* Homewood, Ill.: Business One Irwin.

Shor, Ira. 1992. *Empowering Education.* Chicago: University of Chicago Press.

Shuster, David. 1990. *Teaming for Quality Improvement.* Englewwod Cliffs, N.J.: Prentice-Hall.

Simmons, John. 1990. "Participatory Management: Lessons from the Leaders." *Management Review* (December): 54–58.

Simmons, Robert. 1995. "Control in an Age of Empowerment." *Harvard Business Review* (March-April): 80–88.

Somers, Ken. 1993. "Defining the Boundaries of Empowerment." *Tapping the Network Journal* (Spring): 3–7.

Struebing, Laura. 1996. "Measuring for Excellence." *Quality Progress* (December): 25–28.

Sulzer-Azaroff, Beth, and Harshbarger, Dwight. 1995. "Putting Fear to Flight." *Quality Progress* (December): 61–65.

Sundstrom, Eric, et al. 1990. "Work Teams: Applications and Effectiveness." *American Psychologist* (February): 120–133.

Thor, Carl. 1990. "A Complete Organizational Measurement System." *International Productivity Journal* (Spring): 21–26.

Tjosvold, Dean. 1986. *Working Together to Get Things Done.* Lexington, Mass.: Lexington Books.

Trist, Eric L., et al. 1963. *Organizational Change.* London: Tavistock Press.

Turner, Nathan W. 1977. *Effective Leadership in Small Groups.* Valley Forge, Penn.: Judson Press.

Uhlfelder, Hellen, ed. 1995. *The Advanced Team Guide.* Atlanta: Miller Howard Consulting Group.

Ukens, Lorraine L. 1997. *Working Together.* San Francisco: Jossey-Bass.

Verespej, Michael. 1990. "When You Put the Team in Charge." *Industry Week* (December): 30–32.

Vogt, Judith, and Murrell, Kenneth. 1990. *Empowerment in Organizations.* San Diego: University Associates.

Watson, Charles. 1979. *Management Development Through Training.* Reading, Mass.: Addison-Wesley.

Weber, Allan J. 1995. "Making Performance Appraisals Consistant with a Quality Environment." *Quality Progress* (November): 65–69.

Weisbord, Marvin. 1992. *Discovering Common Ground.* San Francisco: Berrett-Koehler Publishers.

Weisbord, Marvin. 1987. *Productive Workplaces.* San Francisco: Jossey-Bass.

Wellins, Richard S., et al. 1994. *Inside Teams.* San Francisco: Jossey-Bass.

Whyte, William F., 1951. *Patterns for Industrial Peace.* New York: Harper and Brothers.

Index

About the Author

JOHN ROBERT DEW currently serves as Manager for Mission Success at Lockheed Martin's production facility, Paducah, KY where he is responsible for joint union and management team initiatives. He has consulted with hospitals, city government, military, and other industrial organizations on managing in a team environment.

ISBN 1-56720-228-4

HARDCOVER BAR CODE